12 MONTHS OF FUN!

THE LOBSTER KIDS' GUIDE
TO EXPLORING
OTTAWA-HULL

BY JOHN SYMON
EDITED BY BOB KIRNER

Lobster
Press
Limited

Symon, John, 1958-
The Lobster Kids' Guide to Exploring Ottawa-Hull: 12 Months of Fun!
Text copyright © 1999 by Lobster Press Limited
Illustrations copyright © 1998 by Lobster Press Limited

Published by
Lobster Press Limited
1250 René-Lévesque Blvd. West, Suite 2200
Montréal, Québec H3B 4W8
Tel. (514) 989-3121 · Fax (514) 989-3168
www.lobsterpress.com

Assistant Editor: Kathy Tompkins
Copy Editor: Jane Pavanel
Researcher: Iris Glaser
Cover and Illustrations: Christine Battuz
Icons: Christiane Beauregard
Layout and Design: Olivier Lasser with MR Productions

Distribution: Prologue Inc.
1650 Lionel-Bertrand Blvd.
Boisbriand, Québec J7H 1N7
Tel. (450) 434-0306, 1-800-363-2864 · Fax (450) 434-2627

Canadian Cataloguing-in-Publication Data
Includes index.
ISBN 1-894222-01-6

1. Family recreation—National Capital Region (Ont. and Quebec) 2.
Amusements—National Capital Region (Ont. and Quebec) 3. National
Capital Region (Ont. and Quebec)—Description and travel—
Guidebooks. I. Battuz, Christine II. Kirner, Bob, 1959- III. Title.

FC2783.S94 1999   917.13'84044   C99-900367-4
F1059.5.O9S94 1999

Printed and bound in Canada

Table of Contents

The Lobster Kids' Guide series began, unofficially, in 1993, after I'd moved to Montréal and my first-born was old enough to enjoy his first adventures around town. As my family multiplied and grew, we visited many sites in and around the city, and I kept detailed notes of our outings, paying particular attention to places that held special allure for children. I shared this information with others who were on the lookout for kid-friendly attractions. Over the years my notes became quite voluminous, and I approached Lobster Press about publishing them as a guide for families. Within weeks of its launch in June 1998, *The Lobster Kids' Guide to Exploring Montréal* appeared on *The Gazette*'s best-seller list, where it remained for three months.

From this tremendous success came the question of where to go next. Ottawa-Hull seemed the logical choice. The National Capital Region and Montréal are practically neighbours, and my wife and I and our three young children were already making day trips to the area. For readers who wonder if a tourist can write a worthy guidebook about the nation's capital, the answer is yes, without a doubt. Among the things critics liked about the Montréal book was my perspective as a tourist in my own town.

Between 1998 and 1999, my family and I made countless enjoyable trips to visit sites in Ottawa-Hull and the surrounding area. We discovered a region that has an incredible diversity of attractions, including museums, historical sites, theatre, green spaces—in short, many places where children and parents can learn and play. *The Lobster Kids' Guide to Exploring Ottawa-Hull* is written for families with children ages 1 to 12, however, you don't have to be a kid to use it, just a kid at heart.

Have fun!

JOHN SYMON

Introduction

F ast on the heels of our best-selling *The Lobster Kids' Guide to Exploring Montréal*, Lobster Press is proud to present *The Lobster Kids' Guide to Exploring Ottawa-Hull*, the second in our series of guidebooks that offer information and ideas for exploring Canadian cities with children. We won't keep you long from enjoying this book, but first we want to highlight a few things so you can get the most out of our guide.

Whether you're a parent, a teacher or a tourist, if you're caring for children between the ages of 1 and 12, this book is ideal for you. It's a complete resource of things to do and see with kids in the Ottawa-Hull area, both indoors and out, through all four seasons and for all budgets.

The sites in this guide were visited in 1998-99 and the information given for each has been verified. However, since prices and opening hours are liable to change and roads are sometimes under construction and some sites close their doors, please accept our apologies in advance for any inconveniences you may encounter.

Take a moment to read about the "Lobster Rating System." It was created to let you know what John Symon and his children thought of each site. Some activities and sites weren't rated because they didn't fit all the rating criteria.

Next, familiarize yourself with our icons. We designed them to provide information at a glance and also to give you a smile.

The addresses of sites found on the Québec side of the Ottawa River are given in French with the English translation in brackets. This is to facilitate "getting there," as Québec street names on signs and in city maps are in French. Also, all distances to the sites and activities were determined from Parliament Hill. We think it's a good meeting point for east, west, north and south.

We welcome your comments on this guide. We couldn't include everything that's available for children in Ottawa-Hull, so if you feel that we've missed one of your family's favourite destinations, please contact us and we'll print it in the next edition.

A last word: Please be careful when you and your children visit the sites in this guide. Neither Lobster Press nor John Symon can be held responsible for any accidents you or your family might incur.

Enjoy! And watch for the next four books in our series: The Lobster Kids' Guides to Exploring Vancouver, Toronto, Halifax and Calgary.

FROM THE GANG AT LOBSTER PRESS

The Lobster Rating System

W e thought it would be helpful if you knew what the Symon family thought about the sites in this book before you head off to visit them. John and his wife and three children rated every attraction and activity they visited for its:

☞ enjoyment level for children
☞ learning opportunities for children
☞ accessibility from Parliament Hill
☞ costs and value for money

A one-lobster rating: Good attraction.

A two-lobster rating: Very good attraction.

A three-lobster rating: Excellent attraction.

Not fitting some of the criteria, and subsequently not rated, are green spaces and various similar, nearby or other attractions.

Table of Icons

These facilities and/or activities are represented by the following icons:

Beach		Parking	
Bicycling		Picnic tables	
Birthday parties		Playground	
Bus stop		Restaurant/ snack bar	
Coat check			
Cross-country skiing		Skating	
		Snowshoeing	
Downhill skiing		Swimming	
First aid		Telephone	
Heated chalet		Tobogganing	
Hiking		Toilets	
Ice cream stand		Wheelchair/stroller accessible	
In-line skating			
Information centre		Wildlife watching	

Getting Ready

Once you've planned an activity for the day, why not take a few minutes and prepare for it. Nothing will ruin an outing faster than forgetting something important at home. These helpful suggestions will ensure that your next trip is pleasant for everyone.

☞ Call ahead and verify the site's opening hours and prices.

☞ If you're travelling a considerable distance, pack healthy snacks for everyone.

☞ Remember to bring along liquids.

☞ Pack a road map and a first-aid kit, and be sure that anyone who is taking medication has it with them.

☞ Does anyone get car sick? Bring the Gravol™.

☞ Playing "I Spy," having singsongs and listening to your kids' favourite cassettes while on the road will make the drive more pleasant and delay the inevitable "Are we there yet?"

☞ You already know about packing diapers, wipes and spare clothes. But remember to pack a small toy or two for the baby to play with.

☞ Coloured pencils and scratch pads keep little hands busy on a long drive and while waiting for a restaurant meal.

☞ If you're visiting a park, bring along a Frisbee™, a Hacky Sack™ or a soccer ball.

☞ After a long car ride, take the children to a park before heading to a museum or similar site.

☞ Pack insect repellent, sunscreen, swimsuits, towels and hats if it's summer and you're going to an outdoor site.

☞ Bring extra hats, gloves, scarves, boots and warm coats for outdoor winter activities. Dress in layers, wearing a poly-cotton or other moisture-releasing fabric next to your body. A dab of Vaseline™ applied to cheeks and noses reduces the risk of frostbite—so can running to the nearest canteen for hot chocolate!

Bon voyage!

Getting Around with Young Children

S ome of the sites in this guide are located on expansive grounds and are only accessible on foot. This may be problematic for parents with children in strollers, especially if the walk is over rough terrain. In this guide, sites indicated as being wheelchair accessible are suitable for strollers as well.

TRANSPORTING BABIES

Instead of using a stroller, you might consider carrying your child in a Snugli™. When babies grow out of their Snuglies™ and can hold their heads up properly, they're old enough to be transported in child carrier backpacks. Backpacks are ideal for all types of terrain.

BICYCLING WITH CHILDREN

Today, more and more parents want to include their children on long-distance bicycle rides. If your kids are too young to ride on their own, you can carry them in children's bike seats or in a trailer or trail-a-bike. Used alone or in combination, these accessories provide safe and worry-free bicycling for the entire family. Remember to fit your children with bicycle helmets that have been approved.

CROSS-COUNTRY SKIING WITH SMALL CHILDREN

Even if children lack the technique and stamina to cross-country ski, families can still enjoy a day on the trails using one of two devices for carrying them. A carrier backpack is ideal as long as the adult who is wearing it is a strong skier and avoids steep hills. You can also use a ski trailer. Hiking and bicycle shops carry a variety of makes, but keep your eyes open for quality models such as Scandinavia's Ski-pjulken. Though remember, while the skiers in your party are working up a sweat, any youngster who's in a ski trailer is lying in the cold.

If carrying and hauling your children is wearing you down, maybe it's time to look into cross-country skiing lessons for them. The City of Ottawa offers courses for children, adults and seniors at Mooney's Bay Park. For information, call (613) 247-4883.

CHAPTER 1

LOCAL ATTRACTIONS

There's no shortage of attractions near Ottawa-Hull that offer fun-filled activities for families. Whichever direction you head in, it will be a pathway to discovery and excitement for your children.

A short car ride south (a bit longer by bus) takes you to the Agriculture Museum, complete with cuddly animals your kids will love to meet. Afterward, treat everyone to a tour of Dow's Lake in a pedal boat or canoe. The Rideau Canal, which stretches from the lake to downtown, is a popular destination for families who enjoy bicycling, boating or simply strolling. Bring your skates in winter—the canal turns into an 8,000-metre-long rink. Kids never tire of watching the Changing of the Guard on Parliament Hill, and they'll find no end of adventures and activities at the Canadian Children's Museum just across the river. Other local attractions include the Canadian Museum of Civilization, the Ottawa Locks, Rideau Hall, the National Aviation Museum and the very kid-friendly National Museum of Science and Technology.

Child's Play
THE CANADIAN CHILDREN'S MUSEUM

100, RUE LAURIER (LAURIER ST.)
HULL, QUÉBEC
(819) 776-7000 OR **1-800-555-5621**
WWW.CIVILIZATION.CA/CMC

D on't be surprised if your children spend a whole day in this exciting museum, then want to come back for more. The staff are charming and the exhibits demand extended exploration. There are exotic places to visit such as a pyramid that has a secret passageway and a Mexican house where tortillas and handicrafts are made. Your kids can steer a freighter into port, sit astride a camel, ride on a showy Pakistani tour bus or walk through a rain forest.

Children who like to play computer games won't be disappointed. In the Studio, arts and crafts and storytelling are available. For budding entertainers, the puppet theatre offers an opportunity to put on a

---

☞ **SEASONS AND TIMES**

➛ Summer: May 1—Labour Day, daily, 9 am—6 pm; Thu, 9 am—9 pm; Fri (July 1—Labour Day), 9 am—9 pm.
Winter: Oct 13—Apr 30, Tue—Sun, 9 am—5 pm.

☞ **COST**

➛ Adults $8, seniors $7, youth (13 to 17) $6, children (2 to 12) $3, under 2 free, families $18.
Free on Sundays before noon.
Memberships available.

☞ **GETTING THERE**

➛ By car, take Wellington St. east to Mackenzie Ave. and go north across the Alexandra Bridge to Laurier St. and turn west. The museum is on the left. Pay parking on site ($8 maximum). Free street parking on Sundays (arrive early). Minutes from Parliament Hill.
➛ By public transit, take OC Transpo bus 8 (Albert St.).
➛ By bicycle or foot, use the car directions. It's about a 30-minute walk.

> ☞ **NEARBY**
> → Jacques-Cartier Park.
>
> ☞ **COMMENT**
> → Strollers are available for loan. Diaper-changing facilities and locker rentals. Plan at least a 4-hour visit.

show for a real live audience, and there's a stage for young actors, complete with costumes and props. Don't miss Adventure World in the summer. A life-size tugboat and float plane highlight the enclosed outdoor area, which also provides organized games, workshops and crafts.

The museum is open to kids up to age 14 (adults must accompany children under 10). A range of programs, workshops and day camps (March break and summer) is available, and birthday parties and sleepovers can be arranged. For details, call 776-8281.

Science 101 at the NATIONAL MUSEUM OF SCIENCE AND TECHNOLOGY

1867 St. Laurent Blvd.
Ottawa
(613) 991-3044
WWW.SCIENCE.TECH.NMSTC.CA

Planners had children in mind when they built this museum, where interactive exhibits deal with subjects ranging from transportation to space exploration. Your kids will love walking through the tilted Crazy Kitchen, visiting baby chicks at the incubator or riding virtual spacecraft all the way to Mars. Or they can watch demonstrations on topics such as electricity or time. If the weather is fine, head outside to the Technology Park, where mazes, a rocket, a lighthouse, an observatory and other exhibits are waiting to be explored. When it's time for a break, take advantage of the sandy playground and picnic tables.

The museum has educational programs for children, including free one-hour dance, craft and storytelling sessions for kids ages three to five. Theme birthday parties and sleepovers are offered for 6 to 12-year-olds, and astronomy courses are available for families. In December there is a drop-off day care on Saturday mornings. For information about times and prices, call 991-3053.

☞ SEASONS AND TIMES
→ Summer: May 1—Labour Day, daily, 9 am—6 pm; Fri, until 9 pm. Winter: Labour Day—Apr 30, Tue—Sun, 9 am—5 pm. Closed Christmas Day.

☞ COST
→ Adults $6, seniors and students $5, children (6 to 15) $2, under 6 free, families $12.

☞ GETTING THERE
→ By car, take Elgin St. south to Hawthorne Ave. and go east to Main St. Turn south (its name changes to Smyth Rd.) and continue to St. Laurent Blvd. Look for the rocket. Free parking on site. About 10 minutes from Parliament Hill.
→ By public transit, take OC Transpo Transitway bus 95 east to the St. Laurent Station and transfer to buses 85, 111 or 112. Tell the driver your destination. There is a five-minute walk from the stop.

☞ NEARBY
→Mer Bleue Conservation Area, Carlsbad Forest Reserve, Carlsbad Springs Historic Site.

☞ COMMENT
→ Plan at least a 3-hour visit.

The Pageantry and Pleasures of
RIDEAU HALL

1 SUSSEX DR.
OTTAWA
(613) 998-7113 OR **1-800-465-6890**
WWW.GG.CA

Situated in the midst of 32 hectares of trees, gardens and lawns, Rideau Hall, home to the Governor General of Canada, features summer-long activities that are perfect for kids. The festivities start in late June with the inspection of the Ceremonial Guard. Later that week you can take in the First Changing of the Guard and the Trooping of the Colours or attend the Governor General's Garden Party, an annual event that dates from the 1860s.

Throughout July and August, the Visitor's Centre has daily workshops for children ages 5 to 14. Your kids can design a family coat of arms, try on a bearskin hat, learn how to

☞ SEASONS AND TIMES

➤ Grounds: Year-round, daily,
9 am—one hour before sunset.
Visitor's Centre:
Spring: Mid-May—late June, daily,
10 am—5 pm.
Summer: Late June—late Aug, daily,
9:30 am—5:30 pm.
Fall: Late Aug—late Oct, daily,
10 am—5 pm.
Public skating: Mid-Jan—late-Feb,
weekends, 12 pm—5 pm.

☞ COST

➤ Free.

☞ GETTING THERE

➤ By car, take Wellington St. east to
Sussex Dr. and go north. Rideau Hall
is just past the Rideau River on the
right. Limited free parking on site.
About five minutes from Parliament
Hill.
➤ By public transit, take OC Transpo
bus 3.
➤ By bicycle or foot, follow the car
directions.

march or create their own totem pole or inukshuk (an Inuit stone cairn). When they're done, take a guided tour through Rideau Hall's public rooms, gardens and greenhouses, or visit the grounds, which are the site of late-afternoon concerts

> ☞ **NEARBY**
> ➤ Rideau Falls Park, 24 Sussex Drive—the Prime Minister's residence (not open to visits), Rockcliffe Park.
>
> ☞ **COMMENT**
> ➤ Plan a 3-hour visit.

and cricket matches. Walking and bicycling paths will help you find your way. Shaded tables beside a well-equipped playground offer a nice spot for a picnic.

While tours are available in winter to groups only, there is an outdoor skating rink that is open to the public on weekends. A heated chalet has changing areas and toilets.

Making Ice Cream at
THE AGRICULTURE
MUSEUM

EXPERIMENTAL FARM DR. AT PRINCE OF WALES DR.
OTTAWA
(613) 991-3044
WWW.AGRICULTURE.SMNSTC.CA

Visiting the Agriculture Museum is like going on a country outing without leaving the city. Located minutes from downtown at the Central Experimental Farm, this friendly spot features activities for kids, farming demonstrations and exhibits, animals, ornamental gardens and an arboretum.

☞ SEASONS AND TIMES

➤ Animal barns: Year-round, daily, 9 am–5 pm. Closed Christmas Day.
Exhibits: Mar–Oct, daily, 9 am–5 pm.
Birthday parties: June 1–Sept 4, Wed–Sun, 9 am–2 pm.
Gift shop: May–Oct, daily, 10 am–5 pm.

☞ COST

➤ Farm grounds: Free in winter (Nov–Feb).
Grounds, barns and exhibits: Adults $3, seniors, students and children $2, under 3 free, families $7. Group rates and memberships available.
Wagon rides: Adults $2.50, seniors, students and children $1.50. For dates and times, call 991-3044.

☞ GETTING THERE

➤ By car, take Elgin St. south and cross under Hwy. 417. Access Queen Elizabeth Driveway and follow it to Dow's Lake Pavilion. At Experimental Farm Dr. (formerly National Capital Commission Driveway) turn west. Free parking on site. About 10 minutes from Parliament Hill.
➤ By public transit, take OC Transpo bus 3 to Experimental Farm Dr. and Prince of Wales Dr.
➤ By bicycle, take the Rideau Canal Pathway (west side) to Dow's Lake and pedal west along Experimental Farm Dr.

☞ NEARBY

➤ Dow's Lake Pavilion, Rideau Canal, Hartwells Locks, Carleton University Art Gallery.

☞ COMMENT

➤ Stroller rental (small-wheeled models are difficult to push around the site). Plan at least a 2-hour visit.

The exhibits tackle a range of subjects, from potato growing to building barns. But for many youngsters, they play second fiddle to the animals. Children will meet Eeyore the donkey and all his barnyard friends, including pigs, horses, rabbits and chickens. Helpful staff regularly give hands-on lessons in feeding sheep, milking cows, making ice cream and performing other chores. Afterward, take a wagon ride through the arboretum or visit the arts and crafts and tiny tots rooms. Make sure you see the ornamental gardens, which feature a sunken garden, lilacs and roses.

The museum offers a summer day camp and educational programs that promise fun while learning. It also has facilities for children's birthday parties. Packages include a barn tour, pony ride, craft and more. For information, call 991-3053.

Fun for All Seasons
THE RIDEAU CANAL AND DOW'S LAKE

DOW'S LAKE PAVILION
1001 QUEEN ELIZABETH DR.
OTTAWA
(613) 232-1001
WWW.DOWSLAKE.COM

Historic Rideau Canal is a popular destination for families any time of the year. Built between 1826 and 1832 to link Ottawa and Kingston, the stone-walled waterway boasts a scenic eight-kilometre stretch from the Ottawa Locks to Dow's Lake. Recreational pathways follow both sides of the canal and are used by cyclists, runners, in-line skaters and folks just out for a stroll. Rest stops with benches are located at intervals all along the canal.

If you follow the pathways south you'll arrive at Dow's Lake, where you can treat your kids to a ride in a pedal boat, canoe or kayak (if you're on the eastern path, cross the canal at Hartwells Locks and double back to Dow's Lake

☞ SEASONS AND TIMES

➤ Dow's Lake Pavilion:
Summer: May—Sept, daily, 9 am—9 pm.
Winter: Dec—Mar, daily, 9 am—9 pm.
Recreational pathways: Open until covered with snow.
Skateway: Early Jan—Mar (for ice conditions, call 239-5234).

☞ COST

➤ Dow's Lake Pavilion:
Identification and a $20 refundable deposit are required.
Bicycles, in-line skates: $10 per hour ($30 a day).
Canoes, kayaks: Starting at $9 per half-hour ($25 a day).
Pedal boats: Starting at $11 per half-hour ($25 a day).
Sleighs, skates, cross-country skis, snowshoes: $8 per hour ($25 a day).
Recreational pathways: Free.
Skateway: Free (there are donation boxes).

☞ **GETTING THERE**

➤ By car, take Elgin St. south and cross under Hwy. 417. Access Queen Elizabeth Driveway. and follow it to Dow's Lake Pavilion. Pay parking ($5 maximum) across the street. About 10 minutes from Parliament Hill.

➤ By public transit, take OC Transpo bus 3.

➤ By bicycle, take the Rideau Canal Pathway (west side) to Dow's Lake and follow to the pavilion.

☞ **NEARBY**

➤ Agriculture Museum, Dominion Arboretum, Hartwells Locks, Commissioner's Park, Ottawa Locks, Bytown Museum, National Arts Centre, Carleton University Art Gallery.

Pavilion). The pavilion has restaurants, but many families prefer to picnic under the trees at the Dominion Arboretum nearby.

The fun doesn't stop in winter. Bundle up your kids and take them skating on the canal. The Skateway has nearly eight kilometres of groomed ice. If you don't have your own equipment, rentals of skates, cross-country skis, snowshoes and sleighs are available. You'll also find heated huts between the National Arts Centre and Dow's Lake. During Winterlude (page 212) the canal and lake are home to all sorts of activities, including snow-sculpting competitions and skating shows.

Highflying Fun at
THE NATIONAL
AVIATION MUSEUM

ROCKCLIFFE AND AVIATION PARKWAYS
OTTAWA
(613) 993-2010 OR 1-800-463-2038
CLUCAS@NMSTC.CA
WWW.AVIATION.NMSTC.CA

More than a warehouse of vintage aircraft, the National Aviation Museum makes aeronautics fun for kids through a wide range of educational programs and activities. The museum's centrepiece is an exhibit of 60 or so aircraft (it owns more than 100) that traces aviation from the pioneer era to today. The collection includes biplanes, bush planes and jet fighters. Larger aircraft are parked outside behind the museum.

After your children tire of looking at the planes, steer them to the museum's interactive demonstrations. A highlight is a hangglider simulator that kids

☞ **SEASONS AND TIMES**
➤ Summer: May 1—Labour Day, daily, 9 am—5 pm; Thu, 9 am—9 pm. Winter: Labour Day—Apr 30, Tue—Sun, 10 am—5 pm; Thu, 10 am—9 pm. Open on holiday Mondays.

☞ **COST**
➤ Adults $5, children $1.75, under 6 free, families $10.
Free on Thursdays after 5 pm.
Airplane ride: Between $30 and $60 per person depending on the plane.

☞ **GETTING THERE**
➤ By car, take Wellington St. east to Sussex Dr. and go north (Sussex becomes Rockcliffe Pkwy.) to Aviation Pkwy. The museum is on the left. Free parking on site. About 10 minutes from Parliament Hill.
➤ By public transit, take OC Transpo bus 198.
➤ By bike, follow the car directions. A bike path parallels Rockcliffe Pkwy. for much of the way. Exit just before the underpass.

can pilot. Organized activities and crafts are available and the museum has two playrooms with books and games. Out front are a playground and shaded picnic tables. For a real adventure you can reserve a 30-minute ride in an open-cockpit biplane (summer only).

The museum also holds creative and educational workshops and activities for children's groups that include the chance to sleep over under an airplane wing. For information, call 993-4264.

A Walk Through History at THE CANADIAN MUSEUM OF CIVILIZATION

100, RUE LAURIER (LAURIER ST.)
HULL, QUÉBEC
(819) 776-7000 OR 1-800-555-5621
WWW.CIVILIZATION.CA

There's lots to see and do in this spacious museum, where three floors trace the history of civilization in Canada and around the world. For starters, visit the West Coast native village in the Grand Hall. You'll find a life-size re-creation of traditional longhouses and totem poles, as well as exhibits that feature ceremonial masks, clothing, tools and weapons. Your children will want to investigate the archaeological dig. If you can tear them away, head to Canada Hall to see impressive displays of episodes in Canadian history.

The museum also has exhibits of folk art and contemporary native and Inuit art. There's a postal museum in the building, as well as the Canadian Children's Museum (page 21) and the CINÉPLUS theatre (page 123). Families can enjoy daily activities that include crafts and demonstrations for children. Schedules of weekly events are available at the Information Desk near the main entrance.

☞ **SEASONS AND TIMES**

➤ Summer: May 1—Oct 15, daily, 9 am—6 pm; Thu, 9 am—9 pm; Fri (July 1—Labour Day), 9 am—9 pm.
Winter: Oct 16—Apr 30, Tue—Sun, 9 am—5 pm; Thu, until 9 pm. Closed Christmas and New Year's days.

☞ **COST**

➤ Summer: Adults $8, seniors $7, youth (13 to 17) $6, children $3, under 2 free, families (maximum five people) $18.
➤ Winter: Adults $5, seniors and youth $4, children $3, under 2 free, families (maximum five people) $15. Free on Sundays before noon. Memberships available.
Fees for some activities.

☞ **GETTING THERE**

➤ By car, take Wellington St. east to Mackenzie Ave. and go north across the Alexandra Bridge to Laurier St. and turn west. The museum is on the left. Pay parking on site ($8 maximum). Free street parking on Sundays (arrive early). Minutes from Parliament Hill.
➤ By public transit, take OC Transpo bus 8 (Albert St.).
➤ By bicycle or foot, use the car directions. It's about a 30-minute walk.

☞ **NEARBY**

➤ Jacques-Cartier Park.

☞ **COMMENT**

➤Strollers and wheelchairs are available for loan at the cloakroom. Diaper-changing facilities and locker rentals. Plan a half-day visit.

The House on the Hill
PARLIAMENT HILL

WELLINGTON ST. (BETWEEN BANK ST. AND ELGIN ST.)
OTTAWA
(613) 239-5000/992-4793 OR 1-800-465-1867
INFO@NCC-CCN.CA
WWW.PARL.GC.CA OR WWW.CAPCAN.CA

Historic and picturesque, Parliament Hill is the seat of the Canadian government and a must-see for visitors to Ottawa. Built between 1859 and 1866 in the Gothic style, the Hill contains the Centre Block (rebuilt after a fire in 1916) and the East and West blocks that flank it. The Centre Block incorporates the Peace Tower, the Parliamentary Library, the House of Commons and the Senate. Guided tours of the Centre and East blocks are offered daily, and while the tours are geared to adults, older children generally enjoy them.

☞ **SEASONS AND TIMES**
→ Centre Block tours:
Summer: Victoria Day—Labour Day, Mon—Fri, 9 am—7:50 pm; weekends and holidays, 9 am—4:50 pm.
Winter: Labour Day—Victoria Day, daily, 9 am—3:50 pm.
East Block tours:
Early July—Labour Day, daily, 10 am—5:15 pm.
No tours on Canada Day, Christmas Day or New Year's Day.
For group reservations (10 or more), call 996-0896.

☞ **COST**
→ Free.

Younger children are happier taking the shorter, self-guided tour outside. They can watch the Changing of the Guard (daily in the summer at 10 am), visit the Centennial Flame and meet costumed interpreters who will chat with them about Parliament Hill's history. Everyone will appreciate the views from the Peace Tower. Its observation deck is 20 storeys high, offering visitors a look at the entire National Capital Region. Animal lovers may want to take a few minutes to visit the sanctuary for stray cats located behind the Centre Block.

The Peace Tower's carillon performs hour-long concerts weekdays in summer at 2 pm, and outdoor music-and-light shows are given nightly (for details, call 239-5000). Canada Day celebrations on the Hill feature concerts, fireworks and other festivities, and at Christmas you won't want to miss seeing the buildings lit up at night or the beautifully decorated Centre Block.

Tickets for tours and brochures for self-guided visits are available at the white Infotent (daily, mid-May—Labour Day), and at other times at the Visitor Welcome Centre in the Centre Block.

☞ **GETTING THERE**
➤ Car parking is not permitted on the Hill, however, pay parking lots are located nearby.
➤ By public transit, take OC Transpo buses 1, 2, 4 or 7.

☞ **NEARBY**
➤ Capital Infocentre, Canadian Museum of Contemporary Photography, Rideau Canal, Confederation Park, National Archives, National Library, National War Memorial, Supreme Court of Canada.

☞ **COMMENT**
➤ In summer, refreshments are available at the West Block Courtyard. Plan a 2-hour visit.

Picnicking by
THE OTTAWA LOCKS

BETWEEN THE CHÂTEAU LAURIER AND THE OTTAWA RIVER
(613) 283-5170 OR 1-800-230-0016
PARKSCANADA.PCH.GC...U-CANAL/RIDEAU-CANALE.HTM

T he Ottawa Locks is a picturesque ladder of
eight gates situated between the Ottawa River
and the Château Laurier. It is one of 24 lock
stations that are located along the 202-kilometre

☞ **SEASONS AND TIMES**
➥ Victoria Day—October 13.

☞ **COST**
➥ Free.

☞ **GETTING THERE**
➥ By car, take Wellington St. east and park near the Château Laurier
(parking can be difficult to find). It's a short walk from there.
➥ By public transit, take OC Transpo buses 1 through 7.
➥ By bike, take the Rideau Canal Pathway north, or access the locks from
the north end of Major's Hill Park.
➥ By foot, walk east on Wellington St. and descend the stairs from the
bridge that lead to the canal. Walk north for a few minutes.

☞ **NEARBY**
➥ Bytown Museum, Parliament Hill, Major's Hill Park, National Gallery of
Canada, Royal Canadian Mint, Canadian War Museum, Confederation
Park, National War Memorial.

☞ **COMMENT**
➥Operated by Canadian Heritage, Parks Canada.

☞ **SIMILAR ATTRACTIONS**
➥Hartwells and Hog's Back locks (just south of Dow's Lake).

Rideau Canal, and like most locks, its gates are still opened and closed manually by a lock master.

On a summer day you can picnic at tables near the lock station and watch as pleasure craft of all shapes and sizes ply the canal. There's something fascinating about watching the sluice gates swing shut behind a boat that's moving upstream. Once the gates are closed, water pours down from the lock above. When the water level is even with the upstream lock, the lock master opens the next gate to let the boat move on. It takes about 15 minutes for a boat to pass through each gate.

CHAPTER 2

museums

For a family outing that's educational and loads of fun, go to one of Ottawa's many museums. Most offer a fantastic variety of sights and activities that have been designed with kids in mind. Your children will learn about photography, money, nature, local heritage, art, war, history and just about everything else as they explore life-size exhibits, take in dynamic displays, watch films, play computer games and participate in interactive activities. Several of the museums also have workshops and courses for children.

This chapter tells you all you need to know about these kid-friendly museums. Choosing among them won't be easy, so you might as well think of your first museum outing as just the beginning . . . and plan for many more down the road.

NOTE
The following museums, which are covered elsewhere in this guide, also welcome children.

Creating Art at the NATIONAL GALLERY OF CANADA

380 SUSSEX DR.
OTTAWA
(613) 990-1985 OR 1-800-319-2787
INFO@GALLERY.CA
HTTP://NATIONAL.GALLERY.CA

There's something for everyone and a lot for kids at the National Gallery of Canada. For visitors with an interest in architecture, the building itself, which was designed by Moshe Safdie, is spectacular. Inside you'll discover the finest collection of Canadian and European paintings in the country. There are also permanent exhibits of Asian, Inuit and contemporary art, as well as prints, drawings and photographs.

If you're feeling inspired, visit the Artissimo art cart and create your own masterpiece. Located in the Great Hall, it's packed with free art supplies for the whole family. An attendant is on hand to demonstrate such art-making techniques as painting, sculpting and stencilling daily between

☞ **SEASONS AND TIMES**
➤ Summer: May—Oct, daily, 10 am—6 pm; Thu, 10 am—8 pm.
Winter: Oct—Apr, Wed—Sun, 10 am—5 pm; Thu, 10 am—8 pm.

☞ **COST**
➤ Permanent collection: Free.
Special exhibits: Call the gallery for prices.
Group discounts and memberships available.

☞ **GETTING THERE**
➤ By car, take Wellington St. east to Sussex Dr. and turn north to Guigues Ave. Pay parking on site. Minutes from Parliament Hill.
➤ By public transit, take OC Transpo buses 3 or 306.
➤ By bicycle or foot, follow the car directions. It's a pleasant 10-minute walk.

☞ **NEARBY**

➤ Parliament Hill, Royal Canadian Mint, Rideau Hall, Canadian War Museum, Major's Hill Park, Peacekeeping Monument.

☞ **COMMENT**

➤ Strollers and wheelchairs for loan at the information desk. Diaper-changing facilities and bank machines. Plan a 3-hour visit.

1 pm and 4 pm in the summer and on winter weekends.

The gallery has one-hour workshops in sculpting and painting for children ages four to seven who are accompanied by an adult, and for youths eight and up. Registration is held one month before each session and spaces are limited. There is also a range of educational programs for kids of all ages, from pre-schoolers to teens, that includes tours and creative workshops. For more information, call 993-4339. Free noon-hour concerts for children are offered in the outdoor amphitheatre on Thursdays throughout July and August. Bring your lunch.

Natural Wonders
CANADIAN MUSEUM OF NATURE

240 McLeod St.
Ottawa
(613) 566-4700 or 1-800-263-4433
emccrea@mus-nature.ca
http://www.nature.ca

Whether they're interested in animals, plants or minerals, children will love this museum. Dinosaur Hall has life-size skeletons of ancient beasts, including a sabre-toothed tiger, as well as a sand pit for digging fossils. At the Mineral Gallery, where gems and precious metals are on display, there's a re-created gold mine just waiting to be explored. If your kids want to conduct scientific experiments, go to the Exploration Station, which also has activities for adults.

But there's much more to this museum, where four floors are packed with bird and mammal dioram-as, audiovisual presenta-tions, interactive nature games and children's craft tables. Families can take part in special events and activities such as field trips. There are also weekly sessions of music, games and crafts for the younger crowd (ages 3 to 5), and day camps for 6 to 10-year-olds (call 566-4701).

☞ **SEASONS AND TIMES**
➤ Summer: May 1—Sept 7, daily, 9:30 am—5 pm; Thu, until 8 pm. Winter: Sept 8—Apr 30, Tue—Sun, 10 am—5 pm; Thu, until 8 pm. Open holiday Mondays. Closed Christmas Day.

☞ **COST**
➤ Adults $5, seniors and students $4, children (3 to 12) $2, under 3 free, families $12.
Thursdays: Half-price all day, free after 5 pm.
Memberships available.

☞ **GETTING THERE**
➤ By car, take Elgin St. south to McLeod St. and go west one block. Pay parking on site. Minutes from Parliament Hill.
➤ By public transit, take OC Transpo buses 5, 6, 14 or 99.
➤ By bicycle or foot, follow the Rideau Canal Pathway (west side) to McLeod St. and go west. It's about a 30-minute walk from Parliament Hill.

☞ **NEARBY**
➤ St. Luke Park, Minto Park, Rideau Canal.

☞ **COMMENT**
➤ Diaper-changing facilities. Plan a 3-hour visit.

Children's birthday parties can be arranged (ages 5 to 9), as can sleepovers. For details, call 566-4776.

Trooping through the CANADIAN WAR MUSEUM

330 SUSSEX DR.
OTTAWA
(819) 776-8600 OR 1-800-555-5621
WWW.CIVILIZATION.CA

Summer is a good time for kids to visit this museum. If weather permits, they can take in a scuba-diving performance, investigate a Sea King helicopter, clamber over an army tank, then tuck into a well-deserved snack under a camouflaged tent.

There's lots to do inside too. The museum has three floors of narrative and interactive exhibits that trace Canada's wartime history, starting with the fall of New France. Weapons, medals, vehicles and other memorabilia are on display. While some exhibits are beyond the understanding of young children, everyone can relate to the re-created World War I trench, where visitors take a walk-through and try on a gas mask. At the Discovery Room, children will find uniforms, helmets, drums

☞ **SEASONS AND TIMES**
➤ Summer: May 1—mid-Oct, daily, 9:30 am—5 pm; Thu, until 8 pm.
Winter: Mid-Oct—Apr 30, Tue—Sun, 9:30 am—5 pm; Thu, until 8 pm.

☞ **COST**
➤ Adults $4, students and seniors $3, children (2 to 12) $2, under 2 free, family (maximum five people) $9. Group rates available.
Free Sunday mornings for the public; free anytime for Canadian veterans and their families.

☞ **GETTING THERE**
➤ By car, take Wellington St. east to Sussex Dr. and go north. Street parking can be difficult to find. Minutes from Parliament Hill.
➤ By public transit, take OC Transpo buses 3 or 306.
➤ By bicycle or foot, use the car directions. It's about a five-minute ride.

and other military items to play with. Art supplies are also available here.

The museum presents concerts, war films and periodic historical re-enactments. It also has educational programs for students in grades 4 to 12. Guided tours are offered daily. For information, call 776-8606.

☞ **NEARBY**
➤ National Gallery of Canada, Major's Hill Park, Royal Canadian Mint, Peacekeeping Monument.

☞ **COMMENT**
➤ Diaper-changing facilities. Plan a 2-hour visit.

☞ **SIMILAR ATTRACTION**
➤ The Canadian War Museum displays tanks, artillery and a one-man submarine between June and August at Vimy House. Opening hours vary. 221 Champagne Ave. N., Ottawa (819) 776-8600.

Picture Perfect
CANADIAN MUSEUM OF CONTEMPORARY PHOTOGRAPHY

1 RIDEAU CANAL
OTTAWA
(613) 990-8257
CMCP@NGC.CHIN.GC.CA
HTTP://CMCP.GALLERY.CA

I f you like photography and want to stay current on contemporary Canadian photographers, this is the museum to visit. Built in a former railway tunnel, it opened in 1985 and stages several

☞ **SEASONS AND TIMES**
→ Summer: May 1—Labour Day, Mon—
Tue and Fri—Sun, 11 am—5 pm; Wed—
Thu, 11 am—8 pm.
Winter: Day after Labour Day—Apr 30,
Wed and Fri—Sun, 11 am—5 pm; Thu,
11 am—8 pm.
Family Sundays: 1 pm—4 pm.
Closed Christmas and New Year's
days.

☞ **COST**
→ Regular visits: Free (donation
requested).
Family Sundays: $5 per family.

☞ **GETTING THERE**
→ By car, use the walking directions.
Parking is difficult to find.
→ By foot, take Wellington St. west to
the Château Laurier. The museum is
located between the hotel and the
Rideau Canal. It's about a five-
minute walk from Parliament Hill.
→ By public transit, take OC Transpo
buses 1 through 7, 14, 16, 18 or 316.

☞ **NEARBY**
→ Parliament Hill, Bytown Museum,
Ottawa Locks, Major's Hill Park.

☞ **COMMENT**
→ Affiliated with the National Gallery
of Canada. Plan a 30-minute visit
(regular visit).

shows over the course of a
year. Family Sundays are
the best time to visit with
younger children. The
three-hour sessions, which
are offered once a month
from October to May, are
organized by theme and
feature a variety of activities, including magicians,
storytelling and music.

During a regular visit,
ask for an activity booklet
for self-guided tours.
Geared to kids between
the ages of 6 and 12, it
contains questions about
the pictures in the show.
School groups will be
interested in the educa-
tional tours and work-
shops offered to students
in grade 2 and higher. For
details, call 998-0466.

Counting Beans at the CURRENCY MUSEUM

245 SPARKS ST.
OTTAWA
(613) 782-8914
WWW.BANK-BANQUE-CANADA.CA

I f you don't believe that money grows on trees, visit the Currency Museum. You'll learn that in tropical America, people once used cocoa beans like we use cash. There are also many other items to see that have functioned as currency throughout the ages.

Seven galleries display such interesting artifacts as teeth, fish hooks, grain, paper and metal. Think a pocketful of loonies is heavy? Check out the huge stones—they measure two metres across—the Yap peoples traded with in the South Pacific. You can also view exhibits that trace the development of money in Canada from our prehistory to present day. Featured are displays of beaver pelts, seashells and strings of glass beads once used by aboriginal peoples and reproductions of playing

☞ **SEASONS AND TIMES**
➤ Summer: May 1—Labour Day, Mon—Sat, 10:30 am—5 pm; Sun, 1 pm—5 pm.
Winter: Sept—Apr 30, Tue—Sat, 10:30 am—5 pm; Sun, 1 pm—5 pm.

☞ **COST**
➤ Free from July 1 to Labour Day and every Tuesday.
Other times: Individuals $2, children under 8 free, families $5.

☞ **GETTING THERE**
➤ The Bank of Canada building, which houses the Currency Museum, is about a 10-minute walk from Parliament Hill. Heading west, follow the Sparks St. Pedestrian Mall, a lively commercial walkway that in summer is often frequented by jugglers, musicians and other buskers. Continue for three blocks until Metcalfe St.
➤ By public transit, take OC Transpo buses 1, 2, 4, 7, 16 or 18.

☞ **NEARBY**
➤ National Archives, National Library of Canada, Supreme Court of Canada.

☞ **COMMENT**
➤ No diaper-changing facilities. Restaurants nearby. Plan a 1-hour visit.

cards from New France signed by the governor in 1714. There is also an extensive collection of rare Canadian coins and bank notes.

Primarily narrative, the well-presented displays will hold most youngsters' attention only for a short while. More interesting to them will be the Discovery Room, a corner for children that is packed with interactive displays, arts and crafts materials, games and dress-up costumes.

Days of Yore
NEPEAN MUSEUM

16 ROWLEY AVE.
NEPEAN
(613) 723-7936
NMCHIN@TRAVEL-NET.COM
WWW.NEAPEANMUSEUM.ON.CA

Your kids will learn about local history in this small but welcoming museum. A variety of exhibits trace Nepean's evolution, beginning in the early 1790s. You'll find furnishings, clothing, archival photos and tools. The Discovery Gallery, which is designed to look like a turn-of-the-century general store, is particularly popular. It has a bronze cash register, weigh scales and period clothing to dress up in. Kids are invited to use the art supplies and the computer, which has historical guessing games.

Schools can choose from a range of in-class workshops (for grades 1 to 8), where museum staff lead the students in making beeswax candles and identifying artifacts. There are also slide presentations. Heritage Outreach Kits, including a hand-crank ice cream maker, are available for loan. Birthday parties can be arranged.

☞ **SEASONS AND TIMES**
➤ Year-round: Tue—Fri, 10 am—4 pm; weekends, 1 pm—4 pm. Closed between Christmas and New Year's.

☞ **COST**
➤ Visits: Free.
Workshops: $1.50—$3 per student ($.50 extra for non-residents).
Outreach kits: $15 to $25 a week.
Birthdays: $6 per child (minimum of 10 children).

☞ **GETTING THERE**
➤ By car, take O'Connor St. south and follow the signs to Hwy. 417 W. Take Exit 126 (Maitland Ave.) south to Meadowlands Dr. and go west to Rowley Ave. Turn north. The museum is on the left. Free parking on site. About 15 minutes from Parliament Hill.
➤ By public transit, take OC Transpo buses 16 or 18 west on Albert St. to Tunney's Pasture. Transfer to the 86 bus and tell the driver your destination.
➤ By bicycle, take the Rideau Canal Pathway (east side) to Hog's Back Rd. and go west (it becomes Meadowlands Dr.) to Rowley Ave.

☞ **COMMENT**
➤ Plan a 1-hour visit.

Cool Running
CANADIAN SKI
MUSEUM

1960 SCOTT RD., #202
OTTAWA
(613) 722-3584

From cross-country pioneer Jackrabbit Johannsen to Olympic champion Nancy Greene, Canada has produced its share of great skiers. If you're a ski buff, you'll want to learn about these heroes and others in this small museum, which also traces skiing from its beginnings in Europe around 3000 BC to its introduction into Canada in the last century. There's a reproduction of a 5,000-year-old cave drawing from Norway depicting people on skis. Equipment dating back to the 1890s, including barrel staves and birch bindings, is on display, as well as examples of more modern parapher-nalia. The self-guided tours are aided by bilingual explanatory panels. While older kids who love the slopes will get a kick out of seeing how skiing

☞ **SEASONS AND TIMES**
➻ Year-round: Mon—Sat, 9 am—5 pm; Sun, 11 am—5 pm.

☞ **COST**
➻ Free (donation requested).

☞ **GETTING THERE**
➻ By car, take Wellington St. west (it merges with Scott St.) and continue to Clifton St. The museum is located above the Trailhead Ski Shop on the corner of Clifton. Enter through the side door, then climb a flight of stairs. Free parking on site. About 15 minutes from Parliament Hill.
➻ By public transit, take OC Transpo buses 95, 96 or 97 on Albert St. to the Westboro Station. The museum is a short walk east.

☞ **COMMENT**
➻ Operated by volunteers. This site is not accessible to wheelchairs. Plan a 30-minute visit.

evolved, toddlers won't find the narrative exhibits interesting for long.

Basketball Heaven
NAISMITH MUSEUM & HALL OF FAME

14 Bridge St.
Almonte
(613) 256-0492
naismith@trytel.com

How many people know that Dr. James Naismith, born in 1861 in Almonte, Ontario, invented the game of basketball? He achieved this moment of genius in Springfield, Massachusetts, in 1891. The Naismith Museum & Hall of Fame celebrates the man and his legacy with displays that include personal artifacts from his school years and family life. These are supported by biographical panels.

The Canadian Basketball Hall of Fame is also located in the building. It proudly presents a collec-

☞ **SEASONS AND TIMES**
➤ Year-round: Mon—Fri, 9 am—5 pm; weekends, noon—5 pm. (These times are tentative, so call before going.)

☞ **COST**
➤ Adults $3, seniors and children $2.

☞ **GETTING THERE**
➤ By car, take O'Connor St. to Hwy. 417 and go west. Take Exit 155 to Regional Road 49 W. (formerly Hwy. 44 W.) and continue to Almonte. Turn south on Martin St., then west onto Queen St. After crossing the bridge, look for the museum on the left. Free parking on site. About 45 minutes from Parliament Hill.

☞ **COMMENT**
➤ Operated by the Naismith Foundation. Plan a 1-hour visit.

tion of uniforms, signed basketballs, medals, photos, documents and other memorabilia from Canada's basketball giants. Guided tours are available for groups of 10 or more. The Naismith Foundation runs an educational centre at nearby Naismith Farm, where kids up to 16 years of age can attend basketball camp.

Other Museums

Ottawa Art Gallery

2 DALY AVE. (ARTS COURT)
OTTAWA
(613) 233-8699
WWW.CYBERUS.CA/~OAG

H oused in Arts Court, which was the county court-house in the 1870s, the Ottawa Art Gallery show-cases contemporary paintings by local, regional and national artists. New paintings are often on view as the

☞ Year-round: Tue, Wed, Fri, 10 am—5 pm; Thu, 10 am—8 pm; weekends, noon—5 pm.

☞ Free.

☞ Take Wellington St. east to Sussex Dr. and go south. Turn east on Daly Ave. Street parking. About 5 minutes from Parliament Hill.

☞ Take OC Transpo buses 1 through 7, 14, 16 or 18 to the Rideau Mall Station, then walk south to Daly Ave.

exhibits are rotated frequently. There is also a permanent collection, which has works from the Firestone Collection of Canadian Art, including paintings by members of the Group of Seven. If you see a painting you like you may be able to purchase or rent it. Check at the rental desk across from reception.

SIMILAR ATTRACTIONS

☞ **Galerie Montcalm**
Maison de citoyen
25, rue Laurier (Laurier St.) · Hull, Québec · (819) 595-7488

☞ **Centre d'exposition l'Imagier**
9, rue Front (Front St.) · Aylmer, Québec · (819) 684-1445

Museum of Canadian Scouting

1354 BASELINE RD.
OTTAWA
(613) 224-5131

This small museum is a paradise for current and former Beavers, Cubs and Scouts, not to mention children who are eager to embark on the adventure. Located in the lobby of the Scouts Canada building, it features exhibits that trace the history of scouting in Canada. You will find archival books, as well as photos and letters

☞ Year-round: Mon—Fri, 9 am—4:30 pm.

☞ Free.

☞ Take O'Connor St. south and follow the signs for Hwy. 417 and go west. Take Exit 126 (Maitland Ave. S.) and continue to Clyde Ave. and go south. Turn east on Baseline Rd. and look for the totem pole on your left. Free parking on site. About 15 minutes from Parliament Hill.

☞ Take OC Transpo buses 96 or 97 from Slater St. to Billings Station. Transfer to the 118 bus (Kanata/Nepean) and tell the driver your destination.

belonging to Lord Baden-Powell, who founded the Boy Scouts in 1907. There are uniforms on display and an impressive variety of badges from Canada and other countries. The Scout Shop has scouting merchandise for sale. Guided tours can be arranged for groups only.

Pinhey's Point

270 PINHEY'S POINT RD.
KANATA
(613) 832-4347 (SUMMER) OR (613) 592-4291 EXT. 295 (YEAR-ROUND)

Located beside the scenic Ottawa River, historic Pinhey Manor invites visitors to step into the past. The restored limestone building, which dates from the 1820s, features exhibits of local history, art displays and a Discovery Room for children. In summer, kids can take part in making ice cream or fresh bread during thematic discovery days. There is also a theatre night and other special attractions. Picnic tables and nature trails are found on the manor's spacious grounds.

☞ Manor House: Late June—Labour Day, Wed—Sun, 10 am—5 pm. Grounds remain open daily.

☞ Free.

☞ Take Hwy. 417 W. and exit at March Rd./Eagleson Rd. in Kanata. Go north on March Rd. Turn right on Dunrobin Rd. and immediately turn right at Riddell Dr. Go left onto 6th Line Rd. and continue to Pinhey's Point Rd. Turn right. Free parking on site. About 35 minutes from Parliament Hill.

CHAPTER 3

In Your NEIGHBOURHOOD

Sometimes you don't need to travel far to find attractions and activities that will interest kids. Some of the best places to take children are in your own neighbourhood, and most cost very little or are free.

This chapter contains a variety of ideas for outings to public markets, bowling alleys, craft shops and other everyday places, where a little imagination can turn even an ordinary trip, such as going to the car wash, into a fun-filled adventure. Have you ever thought of taking your kids to visit the local police or fire station? They'll love it. The telephone numbers and addresses of these and other neighbourhood attractions, including pools, rinks, tennis courts and children's libraries, are provided on the following pages. There's also a listing of some of the Capital Region's more popular and inexpensive family restaurants, as well as the names of children's hair cutters that will not only make your kids look good, but will cut your hair while they're at it.

Places to Paint
YOUR OWN POTTERY

I f your kids need a new medium for expressing their artistic side, take them to a café where they can paint pottery. You can purchase cups, bowls, piggy banks or a variety of ceramic figures, with prices starting at $7 for some of the smaller items. The café supplies the paints and brushes, and voila!, your children will be occupied creatively for an hour or two.

But you'd better put a limit on the number of pieces you're prepared to buy; younger painters tend to finish their chef-d'oeuvres quickly and want to do more. It can get expensive. The café will fire the pottery and you can drop by in a day or two and pick it up.

Ceramic Cafés in Ottawa

GOTTA PAINT
382 RICHMOND RD., OTTAWA
(613) 729-7754

THE MUD OVEN
1065 BANK ST., OTTAWA
(613) 730-0814

If they like the experience, your children might want to participate in a pottery-making workshop. These community centres have a range of courses for youth:

NEPEAN VISUAL ARTS CENTRE
1701 WOODRUFFE AVE.
(613) 727-6652

GLEBE COMMUNITY CENTRE
363 Lorry Greenberg Dr., Ottawa
(613) 564-1058

McNABB COMMUNITY CENTRE
180 Percy St., Ottawa
(613) 564-1070

DOVERCOURT COMMUNITY CENTRE
411 Dovercourt Ave., Ottawa
(613) 798-8950

CRAFTY PLACES

At the Sassy Bead Company, your children can choose from an extensive selection of beads, baubles and other supplies to design their own necklaces, bracelets and barrettes. You can assemble your jewellery at home or at one of the worktables in the shop. Staff are on hand to help when needed. But not all kids are interested in accessories. Fortunately, Sassy's is chock-full of other creative possibilities such as beaded animal figurines to hang from a backpack or keychain.

The shop offers several workshops, including learning the basics of stringing and wiring, making hemp jewellery, and decorating picture frames with Sculpey™ clay. It also hosts birthday parties (in-store or at your home) which include supplies and a staff member who will lead the children in craft making, as well as a prize and a $5 gift certificate for the birthday child.

THE SASSY BEAD COMPANY
757 Bank St. (The Glebe) • (613) 567-7886
11 William St. (ByWard Market) • (613) 562-2812

Other Places to Make Crafts

Many community centres provide arts and crafts instruction to children.

Contact your area school board and ask if local schools have after-hour or weekend art programs.

Other centres where children can express their creativity are listed below and in the General Index under Workshops/Camps/Programs at the back of this book.

NEPEAN VISUAL ARTS CENTRE
1701 WOODROFFE AVE.
(613) 727-6652

NEPEAN CREATIVE ARTS CENTRE
11-35 STAFFORD RD,
(613) 596-5783

OTTAWA SCHOOL OF ART
35 GEORGE ST.
(613) 241-7471

White Rose offers seasonal workshops where kids can make Christmas, Easter and Halloween decorations. Your local craft store might also have courses for children.

WHITE ROSE
150 ROBERTSON RD., NEPEAN • (613) 828-8981
1605 ORLÉANS BLVD., ORLÉANS • (613) 834-6483
2446 BANK ST., OTTAWA • (613) 247-1414

Rainy-day BOWLING ALLEYS

Bowling is an ideal rainy-day activity for kids and their parents. Children as young as two will enjoy playing, albeit by their own rules. Certain alleys in the area cater to families by making lightweight, easy-to-handle balls available for children. At other establishments kids can bowl on bumper lanes (lanes with no gutters), guaranteeing they'll hit the pins every time. Mornings are usually the best time to take the family bowling; the alleys are less crowded then and not as smoky.

☞ **SEASONS AND TIMES**
➤ Year-round: Daily.

☞ **COST**
➤ One game: $2 to $3.
Shoe rental: $1.50 per pair.
Birthday packages: Inquire at the alley.

If your kids enjoy the sport—a game between four friends lasts about 45 minutes—they might want to celebrate their birthdays at the lanes. Staff will tell you what facilities are available for children's parties. Birthday packages may include several games of bowling, shoe rentals, a lunch, a decorated birthday room and a supply of balloons.

There's no shortage of bowling alleys in the National Capital Region. Here's a selection of those offering children's birthday parties:

ALADDIN BOWLING CENTRE
435 DONALD ST., OTTAWA
(613) 744-5552

KANATA KLASSIC BOWL
(FOUR BIRTHDAY PACKAGES AVAILABLE)
80 HINES RD., KANATA
(613) 599-2695

KENT BOWLING LANES
270 CATHERINE ST., OTTAWA
(613) 232-0379

McARTHUR LANES
(NO BIRTHDAY PACKAGES; SPECIAL KIDS' LANES)
175 McARTHUR AVE., VANIER
(613) 745-2117

MERIVALE BOWLING CENTRE
1916 MERIVALE RD., NEPEAN
(613) 228-9190

NORTH GOWER BOWLING ALLEY
6548 FOURTH LINE RD., NORTH GOWER
(613) 489-3873

ORLÉANS BOWLING CENTRE INC.
885 TAYLOR CREEK DR., ORLÉANS
(613) 837-7000

QUEENSWAY BOWL
1401 CARLING AVE., OTTAWA
(613) 729-8500

RA CENTRE
2451 RIVERSIDE DR., OTTAWA
(613) 733-5100

SALLES DE QUILLES D'EMBRUN
8 BLAIS, EMBRUN
(613) 443-3036

VISIONS BOWLING CENTRE
49 BRIDGE ST., CARLETON PLACE
(613) 253-0094

WALKLEY BOWLING CENTRE
2092 WALKLEY RD., OTTAWA
(613) 521-0132

WEST PARK BOWLING
1205 WELLINGTON ST., OTTAWA
(613) 728-0933

QUILL-O-DROME GALAXIE
90, RUE ALBERT, AYLMER
(819) 682-2695

SALLE DE QUILLES MASSON
27 GEORGES, MASSON-ANGERS
(819) 986-3818

Shopping at
A PUBLIC MARKET

The next time you need to shop for fruits and vegetables, consider buying them at a public market. These open-air emporiums offer children the sights and smells of fresh farm produce amidst the hustle and bustle of commercial activity. While the cost of potatoes, cucumbers, strawberries and other fruits grown by Ottawa Valley farmers generally matches supermarket prices, there's no comparing the quality of goods or the atmosphere. You can purchase in-season firewood, maple syrup, Halloween pumpkins and Christmas trees at year-round markets. Jewellery, woollen goods and other hand-crafted items are often sold as well. Some markets, including Ottawa's famous ByWard Market, have seasonal festivals where families can savour a stew cook-off, ogle classic cars or enjoy hot apple cider while listening to carollers.

BYWARD MARKET
BETWEEN YORK ST. AND GEORGE ST.
(613) 244-4410 • (ADMINISTRATION)
OR **(613) 562-3325** • (SEASONAL EVENTS)
☞ Year-round: Daily, 6 am—6 pm.
Closed Christmas and New Year's days.

PARKDALE MARKET
PARKDALE AVE. (BETWEEN WELLINGTON
ST. AND ARMSTRONG ST.)
(613) 244-4410
☞ Year round: Daily, 6 am—
6 pm. Closed Christmas and New
Year's days.

> ☞ **COST**
> ➤ Free to browse. Parking charges
> may apply.
>
> ☞ **COMMENT**
> ➤ Toilets are not usually available at
> public markets. Keep an eye open for
> nearby restaurants.

SPARKS STREET MALL OUTDOOR MARKET
SPARKS ST. (BETWEEN ELGIN ST. AND LYON ST.)
(613) 230-0984
☞ Summers: Daily.

Visiting the Neighbourhood FIRE STATION

F irefighters like showing kids around their stations. Not every station house has a fireman's
pole, but children will get to see gleaming
trucks, rescue equipment, uniforms and other fire-
fighting paraphernalia. While larger fire departments
in the Capital Region generally have an open-door policy, smaller volunteer brigades may not have the staff
on hand to provide tours, so call ahead. Officials from
fire departments often give talks to day cares and school

☞ **SEASONS AND TIMES**
➤ Call your municipal fire department for information.

☞ **COST**
➤ Free.

☞ **COMMENT**
➤ Call ahead to see if your visit will be at a convenient time.

groups about fire prevention. A visit to the station house makes a terrific follow-up.

Kids can have a Sparky tour of Kanata's fire stations, where they'll get to check out the trucks and wear a helmet. Maybe a firefighter will sound a siren. For information, call (613) 836-1046. At Ottawa fire halls, kids can see clothing and equipment, and older children can climb aboard one of the trucks. To arrange a group tour, call (613) 798-8825.

Station No. 1 in Cumberland (500 Charlemagne Blvd.) is open to visits from the public daily, however, groups should call ahead at (613) 824-5777. In addition to giving tours of its fire halls (please phone ahead), the Nepean Fire Department has a fire safety house trailer, complete with hot doors and smoke, that's used to demonstrate fire safety at schools and community events. For more information, call (613) 825-2020. For the administration number (not the emergency number) of your municipal fire department, look in the blue pages of the telephone directory.

Cruising to Your Local
POLICE STATION

F irefighters aren't the only local heroes to set out a welcome mat for the community, especially its youngest members. Thanks to the recent trend toward neighbourhood policing, many police stations have an open-door policy for visitors. It's just the ticket for budding detectives or anyone who's fascinated by flashing lights and wailing sirens.

☞ **SEASONS AND TIMES**
→ Call your local police station for information.

☞ **COST**
→ Free.

☞ **COMMENT**
→ Call ahead to see if your visit will be at a convenient time.
Police officers will also visit schools and community groups. Perhaps your group could host a police-sponsored bicycle safety rodeo or seminar on being street-smart.

Depending on the station, officers will fingerprint your children, let them check out the cells, show them a patrol car or give them road and personal safety tips. While there, ask if an officer will do a car-seat safety inspection on your car. At some stations, engraving pens for marking valuables are available.

Tours of stations in Cumberland, Gloucester, Nepean, Ottawa and Vanier can be arranged through the office of the Chief of Police, (613) 236-1222, extension 5590. OPP detachments in Kanata, (613) 592-6061, Kemptville, (613) 258-3441 and Rockland/ Castleman, (613) 446-5124 can also be visited, as can the RCMP stables in Ottawa (page 138). For the administration number (not the emergency number) of your municipal police department, look in the blue pages of the telephone directory.

THE GREAT CAR WASH ADVENTURE

Every car owner needs to clean their vehicle sooner or later. When that day arrives, why not round up your kids and head to the nearest car wash. While some toddlers are frightened by the thundering of the machinery and the pounding streams of water, most children anticipate the adventure eagerly. It begins with the wait. One by one, the cars ahead of you disappear into the huge, dark entrance. As you inch forward, calling to everyone to batten down the windows and doors, their excitement rises to near fever pitch. The more daring of your children may even undo their seat belts! As for your part, all you have to do is slip the gear into neutral, sit back and enjoy the ride.

☞ **SEASONS AND TIMES**
➤ Year-round, except during winter cold snaps.

☞ **COST**
➤ Minimal when purchasing gas.

☞ **COMMENT**
➤ Generally operated by gas stations. There's probably one in your neighbourhood.

Dining Out at
KID-FRIENDLY RESTAURANTS

D ining out with the family offers two rewards: it's fun and it gives the cook in the household a well-deserved break. But if you have many mouths to feed, it can be expensive. Fortunately, there's no shortage of family restaurants in the National Capital Region where diners can choose from a variety of dishes and expect good value. Better still, these establishments are happy to see kids. Many have children's menus and serve kiddie-size portions. Others provide crayons or offer activities to keep the little ones happy. But before heading out with the troops, call ahead to ask if the restaurant has high-chairs or child boosters.

Au Vieux Duluth
(STEAK AND SEAFOOD; INEXPENSIVE FAMILY DINING)
56-A, BOUL. GRÉBER, HULL • (819) 243-5773
260 CENTRUM BLVD., ORLÉANS • (613) 841-7475
585 MONTREAL RD., OTTAWA • (613) 842-4888

Bagel Bagel
92 CLARENCE ST., OTTAWA • (613) 241-8998

Bangkok Thai Garden
(SOME ITEMS ARE SPICY)
370 DALHOUSIE ST., OTTAWA • (613) 789-1888

Baxter's
(KIDS' MENU; SUNDAY BRUNCH)
1344 BANK ST., OTTAWA • (613) 738-3323

CHANCES R
(KIDS' MENU)
SHOPPER'S CITY WEST (BASELINE AT WOODROFFE), NEPEAN • (613) 225-6887

COWS
(PREMIUM ICE-CREAM TREATS; GIFT SHOP)
43 CLARENCE ST., OTTAWA • (613) 789-2697

CRÊPERIE & MAISON DU SPAGHETTI
(KIDS' MENU)
355, BOUL. GRÉBER, HULL • (819) 561-5290

EAST SIDE MARIO'S
(KIDS' MENU; CRAYONS)
320, BOUL. ST-JOSEPH (LES GALERIES DE HULL), HULL • (819) 776-6607
651 TERRY FOX DR., KANATA • (613) 836-3680
1 STAFFORD RD., NEPEAN • (613) 820-3278
250 CENTRUM BLVD., ORLÉANS • (613) 834-1388
1200 ST. LAURENT BLVD. (ST. LAURENT CENTRE), OTTAWA • (613) 747-0888

GREEN DOOR RESTAURANT
(ORGANIC, VEGETARIAN MENU; CLOSED MONDAYS)
198 MAIN ST., OTTAWA • (613) 234-9597

HY'S STEAK HOUSE
(IF MONEY'S NO OBJECT AND YOU FEEL LIKE CELEBRATING)
170 QUEEN ST., OTTAWA • (613) 234-4545

LICK'S ICE CREAM & BURGER SHOP
1788 BANK ST., OTTAWA • (613) 738-9606

MEXICALI ROSA'S
(TEX-MEX; KIDS' MENU)
1100, BOUL. MALONEY OUEST, HULL • (819) 243-1610
2401 ST. JOSEPH BLVD., ORLÉANS • (613) 824-6014
DOW'S LAKE PAVILION, OTTAWA • (613) 234-8156
895 BANK ST., OTTAWA • (613) 236-9499
975 RICHMOND RD., OTTAWA • (613) 722-4692
200 RIDEAU ST., OTTAWA • (613) 241-7044

NICKELS
(DINER FOOD AND ATMOSPHERE; KIDS' MENU; CRAYONS)
655 TERRY FOX DR., KANATA • (613) 836-2025
519 WEST HUNT CLUB (AT MERIVALE), NEPEAN • (613) 225-8665
128 GEORGE ST., OTTAWA • (613) 562-9865

PIZ'ZA-ZA CAFÉ RESTAU
(ITALIAN)
36, RUE LAVAL, HULL • (819) 771-0565

RED LOBSTER
1499 ST. LAURENT BLVD., OTTAWA • (613) 744-7560

RESTAURANT BARBE
122, RUE EDDY, HULL • (819) 777-7384

ROCKWELL'S
(ALL-DAY BREAKFAST)
1642 MERIVALE RD. (MERIVALE MALL), NEPEAN • (613) 224-8135

RÔTISSERIES AU COQ
(CHICKEN)
755, BOUL. ST-JOSEPH, HULL • (819) 778-0880

RÔTISSERIE ST-HUBERT
(CRAYONS WHILE YOU WAIT; KIDS' MENU)
181, RUE PRINCIPALE, AYLMER • (819) 685-9119
357, BOUL. MALONEY OUEST, GATINEAU • (819) 643-4419
225, BOUL. MAISONNEUVE, HULL • (819) 776-6012
2484 ST. JOSEPH BLVD., ORLÉANS • (613) 824-3267
1480 RICHMOND RD., OTTAWA • (613) 820-8702
1754 ST. LAURENT BLVD., OTTAWA • (613) 526-1222

SOUTHERN CROSS
(TEX-MEX AND SOUTHERN; KIDS' MENU)
402 QUEEN ST. (IN THE TRAVELODGE), OTTAWA • (613) 230-0400

SWISS CHALET
(KIDS' MENU; CRAYONS AND SMALL TOYS)
2808 ST. JOSEPH BLVD., ORLÉANS • (613) 830-9128

ZAK'S DINER
(KIDS' MENU; BIRTHDAY PARTIES; ALL-DAY BREAKFAST)
777 BANK ST., OTTAWA • (613) 232-9257
16 BYWARD MARKET, OTTAWA • (613) 241-2401

For something different try a buffet. Kids love choosing their own dishes.

BUFFET INDIA
1370 CLYDE AVE., NEPEAN • (613) 225-3009

DU BARRY BUFFET CHINOIS/CHINESE BUFFET
343, BOUL. GRÉBER, HULL • (819) 568-2088
33 SELKIRK ST., VANIER • (613) 749-2088

FOODY GOODY
(CHINESE BUFFET; KIDS' PRICES; WEEKEND BRUNCH)
3825 RICHMOND RD., BELL'S CORNERS • (613) 596-2828

VEER PREET
(INDIAN BUFFET)
2181 ST. JOSEPH BLVD., ORLÉANS • (613) 830-7458

Need to manage your time better? You can eat while doing the laundry at:

LAVA JAVA WASH HOUSE AND BEAN EMPORIUM
(COFFEE SHOP)
124 OSGOODE ST., OTTAWA
(613) 565-9274

WRINGER'S LAUNDROMAT-RESTAURANT
151-B SECOND AVE., OTTAWA
(613) 234-9700

These popular fast-food restaurants have outlets located throughout Ottawa-Hull. Check the telephone directory for the one that's most convenient for you (kids' menus; toys).

BURGER KING

HARVEY'S

McDONALD'S (PARTIAL LISTING ON PAGE 101)

SUBWAY

TACO BELL

WENDY'S

Combing the Area for
CHILDREN'S HAIR CUTTERS

F or some children having a first haircut can be as upsetting as visiting the doctor or dentist. You can ease their fears and dry their tears by taking them to a hair cutter that caters to kids.

First Choice Haircutters' outlets service the whole family. Kids are given a toy-of-the-month when they're finished. The toy is also available to siblings who've come along but aren't having their hair cut that day.

GLOUCESTER
2515 BANK ST. (SOUTHGATE MALL) • (613) 526-4962
1247 DONALD ST. • (613) 748-6565
2187 OGILVIE RD. • (613) 744-3382

KANATA
442 HAZELDEAN RD. • (613) 831-0969
700 MARCH RD. • (613) 599-5698

NEPEAN
3500 FALLOWFIELD RD. • (613) 823-3357
1541 MERIVALE RD. (AT CAPILANO DR.) • (613) 225-8104
1 STAFFORD RD. E. (BELL'S CORNERS) • (613) 828-4832

ORLÉANS
250 CENTRUM BLVD. • (613) 834-1660
5929 JEANNE D'ARC BLVD. • (613) 837-7942

OTTAWA
1717 BANK ST. • (613) 523-1727
1867 CARLING AVE. • (613) 728-7794
1460 RICHMOND RD. • (613) 820-0741

STITTSVILLE
1300 MAIN ST. (STITTSVILLE SHOPPING CENTRE) • (613) 831-3039

VANIER
EAST VIEW SHOPPING MALL • (613) 745-4698
355 MONTREAL RD. (CLOSED SUN) • (613) 745-5986

RINALDO'S
111 ALBERT ST. (WORLD EXCHANGE PLAZA), OTTAWA • (613) 235-6666

While he doesn't specialize in children's cuts, Rinaldo will pamper your children during their visit to his salon and spa.

Rinaldo is a well-known Ottawa character whose prices for kids' cuts are reasonable, and they will enjoy meeting his adorable dogs. You never know which famous personality might be sitting in the next chair.

Local Treasure Chests
CHILDREN'S LIBRARIES

Visit any municipal library in the National Capital Region and you'll find a children's section. These days they contain more than books and cosy corners. Your kids will also have access to games, toys, videos, music, interactive computers and Internet facilities. You'll be able to choose from an extensive collection of English and French titles, and sometimes books in other languages are available as well. If the library doesn't have a copy of the book your child wants, make an acquisition request at the main desk or ask if they can obtain it on inter-library loan. Many libraries have storytime and other programs for children. Only residents have book-bor-

☞ **SEASONS AND TIMES**
➤ Schedules vary. Some smaller libraries are open just a few days each week.

☞ **COST**
➤ Usually free for residents. Proof of residency may be required—a hydro bill or driver's licence will suffice.

rowing privileges and can use the audio-visual and computer facilities. Non-residents can use the books in the library.

ALMONTE
155 High St. • (613) 256-1037

AYLMER
120, rue Principale • (819) 685-5009

CARLETON PLACE
101 Beckwith St. • (613) 257-2702

CHELSEA LIBRARY
100, ch. Old Chelsea • (819) 827-4019

CUMBERLAND
1599 Tenth Line Rd. • (613) 830-5422

BOOKMOBILE SERVICE
TO CUMBERLAND, NAVAN,
NOTRE-DAME-DES-CHAMPS,
SARSFIELD AND VARS:
(613) 835-2665

GATINEAU
BIBLIOTHÉQUE CENTRALE
BOWATER/AVENOR LIBRARY
855, boul. de la Gappe
(819) 243-2506

DE LA RIVIERA BRANCH
12, rue de Picardie • (819) 243-2543

DOCTOR-JEAN-LORRAIN BRANCH
20, boul. Lorrain • (819) 669-5201

GLOUCESTER
CHILDREN'S PROGRAMMING
(613) 748-4241

BLACKBURN HAMLET BRANCH
199 Glen Park Dr. • (613) 824-6926

BLOSSOM PARK BRANCH
2950 Bank St., Unit 7
(613) 731-9907

GLOUCESTER NORTH BRANCH
2036 Ogilvie Rd. • (613) 748-4208

ORLÉANS BRANCH
1705 Orléans Blvd. • (613) 824-1962

GOULBOURN
MUNSTER BRANCH
7749 Bleeks Rd. • (613) 838-2888

RICHMOND BRANCH
6240 Perth St. • (613) 838-2026

STITTSVILLE BRANCH
1637 Main St. • (613) 836-2522

HULL
BIBLIOTHÉQUE CENTRALE
25, rue Laurier • (819) 595-7460

LUCIEN-LALONDE BRANCH
225, rue Berri • (819) 595-7480

AURÉLIAN-DOUCET BRANCH
207, boul. du Mont-Bleu
(819) 595-7490

KANATA
BEAVERBROOK BRANCH
John Mlacak Centre
2500 Campeau Dr. • (613) 592-2712

HAZELDEAN BRANCH
50 Castlefrank Rd. • (613) 836-1900

NEPEAN
CHILDREN'S PROGRAMMING
(613) 727-6700 ext. 7473/4

CENTRAL LIBRARY
101 Centrepointe Dr.
(613) 727-6649

CENTENNIAL BRANCH (BELL'S CORNERS)
3870 Richmond Rd. • (613) 828-5142

EMERALD PLAZA BRANCH
1547 Merivale Rd. • (613) 224-7874

RUTH E. DICKINSON BRANCH
100 Malvern Dr. • (613) 825-3508

OSGOODE

METCALFE LIBRARY
2782 Albert St. • (613) 821-1330

GREELY LIBRARY
7008 Parkway Rd. • (613) 821-3609

OSGOODE LIBRARY
5630 Main St. • (613) 826-2227

VERNON LIBRARY
4082 Hwy. 31 • (613) 821-3389

OTTAWA

CHILDREN'S PROGRAMMING
(613) 236-0301

BOOKMOBILE • (613) 730-1082

MAIN LIBRARY
120 Metcalfe St. • (613) 236-0301

ALTA VISTA BRANCH
2516 Alta Vista Dr. • (613) 737-2837

CARLINGWOOD BRANCH
281 Woodroffe Ave. • (613) 725-2449

ELMVALE ACRES SHOPPING CENTRE BRANCH
Elmvale Acres • (613) 738-0619

RIDEAU BRANCH
377 Rideau St. • (613) 241-6954

ST. LAURENT BRANCH
515 Côté St. • (613) 748-1531

SOUTH BRANCH
1049 Bank St. • (613) 730-1082

WEST BRANCH
18 Rosemount Ave. • (613) 729-8664

LA PÊCHE

BIBLIOTHÉQUE WAKEFIELD
20, ch. Valley • (819) 459-3266

PONTIAC LIBRARY

Beside the Hôtel de Ville
(819) 455-2370

RIDEAU

MANOTICK LIBRARY
5499 South River Dr.
(613) 692-3854

NORTH GOWER LIBRARY
6579 Fourth Line Rd.
(613) 489-3909

ROCKCLIFFE PARK

380 Springfield Rd. • (613) 745-2562

ROCKLAND

2085 Laurier St. • (613) 446-5680

VAL-DES-MONTS

BIBLIOTHÉQUE ST-PIERRE DE WAKEFIELD
24, ch. du Parc • (819) 457-1911

VANIER

310 des Pères Blancs Ave.
(613) 745-0861

WEST CARLETON

3911 Carp Rd. • (613) 839-5412

Cool Places to Play
SWIMMING POOLS

For kids, the best place to spend a hot summer afternoon is at the local pool. Most community pools, whether indoor or outdoor, have swimming lessons for children of all ages. Other aquatic sports are also frequently available. While some municipal pools refuse entry to babies in diapers, others welcome them. Some even host birthday parties. Here's a listing of the indoor pools around town, as well as the numbers you can call for the locations and schedules of the outdoor pools in your municipality.

CARLETON PLACE
359 Bridge St. • (613) 257-1005

CHELSEA
Chelsea has no pools, but residents can use the ones in Hull. For information, call the Recreation Department:
(819) 827-1843

CUMBERLAND
OASIS WAVE AND LEISURE POOL
Ray Friel Centre
1585 Tenth Line Rd., Fallingbrook • (613) 830-2747

GATINEAU
Gatineau has 13 outdoor pools. For information about their schedules, call the Service des loisirs et de la culture at (819) 243-4343. Indoor swimming is offered to residents at:

ÉCOLE POLYVALENTE DE L'ÉRABLIÈRE
500, rue de Cannes

ÉCOLE POLYVALENTE LE CARREFOUR
50, ch. de la Savane

GLOUCESTER
BEARBROOK POOL (outdoor)
2679 Innes Rd. • (613) 824-8300

ORLÉANS RECREATION COMPLEX
1490 Youville Dr. • (613) 824-0819 ext. 233

SAWMILL CREEK POOL
3380 d'Aoust Ave. • (613) 521-4092

SPLASH WAVE POOL
2040 Ogilvie Rd. • (613) 748-4222

HULL
For the locations and schedules of Hull's outdoor pools and wading pools, call (819) 595-7400. Indoor swimming for Hull residents is available at:

ÉCOLE SECONDAIRE DE L'ÎLE
255, rue Saint-Rédempteur • (819) 595-7400

ÉCOLE SECONDAIRE MONT-BLEU
389, boul. de la Cité-des-Jeunes • (819) 595-7400

COLLÈGE DE L'OUTAOUAIS
333, boul. de la Cité-des-Jeunes • (819) 770-4012

UNIVERSITÉ DU QUÉBEC À HULL
283, boul. Alexandre-Taché • (819) 595-2310

SPORTHÈQUE DE HULL
72, rue Jean-Proulx • (819) 777-5656

KANATA
KANATA WAVE POOL & LEISURE CENTRE
70 Aird Pl. • (613) 591-9283

BEAVERBROOK POOL (outdoor)
2 Beaverbrook Rd. • (613) 592-4291 ext. 247

KATIMAVIK POOL (outdoor)
64 Chimo Dr. • (613) 592-4291 ext. 247

GLEN CAIRN POOL (outdoor)
186 Morrena Rd. • (613) 592-4291 ext. 247

NEPEAN
NEPEAN SPORTSPLEX
1701 Woodroffe Ave. • (613) 727-6665

WALTER BAKER SPORTS CENTRE
100 Malvern Dr. • (613) 727-6700 ext. 7684

OTTAWA
For the locations and schedules of Ottawa's outdoor pools and wading pools, call (613) 244-5678. Indoor swimming is offered at:

BREWER POOL
216 Hopewell Ave. • (613) 247-4938

CANTERBURY POOL
2185 Arch St. • (613) 247-4865

CHAMPAGNE POOL
321 King Edward Ave. • **(613) 244-4402**

CLIFFORD BOWEY POOL
1300 Kitchener Ave. • **(613) 247-4820**

DOVERCOURT POOL
411 Dovercourt Ave. • **(613) 798-8956**

JACK PURCELL POOL
320 Jack Purcell Lane • **(613) 564-1027**

LOWERTOWN POOL
40 Cobourg St. • **(613) 244-4406**

PINECREST POOL
2250 Torquay Ave. • **(613) 828-3118**

ST-LAURENT POOL
525 Côté St. • **(613) 742-6767**

Cool Places to Play II
CITY RINKS

I f you like to strap on skates, you're in luck. There's no shortage of skating rinks in the Capital Region. The indoor rinks are listed here, as well as the numbers to call for the schedules and locations of the outdoor rinks in your neighbourhood. While hockey, figure skating and other organized activities often dominate the ice time, arenas usually set aside several hours each week for free skating. Call your municipal rink for information about its schedule of activities.

ALMONTE AREA
ALMONTE ARENA
182 Bridge St. • **(613) 256 1077**

PAKENHAM ARENA
112 Victoria St., Pakenham • (613) 256-1077

AYLMER
FRANK-ROBINSON ARENA
96, ch. Albert • (819) 685-5008

ISABELLE-ET-PAUL DUCHESNAY ARENA
92, ch. Albert • (819) 685-5008

CARLETON PLACE
75 Neelin St. • (613) 257-1690

CHELSEA
Outdoor rinks only. For locations and times, call (819) 827-1843.

CUMBERLAND TOWNSHIP
RAY FRIEL CENTRE
1585 Tenth Line Rd., Fallingbrook • (613) 830-2747

R. J. KENNEDY MEMORIAL ARENA
1115 Dunning Rd., Cumberland • (613) 833-2375

NAVAN MEMORIAL ARENA
1295 Colonial Rd., Navan • (613) 835-2066

GATINEAU
For the locations and schedules of Gatineau's outdoor rinks, call (819) 243-4344.

BARIBEAU ARENA
444, rue Caron • (819) 669-2570

BEAUDRY ARENA
23, rue St-Alexandre • (819) 243-2542

CAMPEAU ARENA
165, rue des Sables • (819) 669-2560

STADE PIERRE LAFONTAINE
225, rue St-Antoine • (819) 243-2544

LAC BEAUCHAMP PARK ARENA
Lac Beauchamp Park • (819) 243-4343

GLOUCESTER
For the locations and schedules of Gloucester's outdoor rinks, call (613) 748-4100.

MINTO SKATING CENTRE
2571 Lancaster Rd. • (613) 733-7800

BLACKBURN ARENA
200 Glen Park Dr. • (613) 824-5197

EARL ARMSTRONG ARENA
2020 Ogilvie Rd. • (613) 746-7109

ELIZABETH MANLEY RINK
ORLÉANS RECREATION COMPLEX
1490 YOUVILLE DR. • (613) 748-4210

FRED G. BARRETT ARENA
3280 LEITRIM RD. • (613) 822-2175

J. B. POTVIN ARENA
813 SHEFFORD RD. • (613) 741-1537

ORLÉANS RECREATION COMPLEX
1490 YOUVILLE DR. • (613) 748-4210

GOULBOURN TOWNSHIP
RICHMOND MEMORIAL ARENA
6095 PERTH RD., RICHMOND
(613) 838-5423

STITTSVILLE AND DISTRICT ARENA
10 CHURCH ST., STITTSVILLE
(613) 836-5941

HULL
FOR THE LOCATIONS AND SCHEDULES OF HULL'S OUTDOOR RINKS,
CALL (819) 595-7400.

ARÉNA CHOLETTE
156, BOUL. DE LA CITÉ-DES JEUNES • (819) 595-7700

ARÉNA JEAN-PAUL-SABOURIN
70, RUE JEAN-PROULX • (819) 595-7700

ARÉNA ROBERT-GUERTIN
125, RUE CARILLON • (819) 595-7700

KANATA
FOR THE LOCATIONS AND SCHEDULES OF KANATA'S OUTDOOR RINKS,
CALL (613) 592-4291.

JOHN F. MLACAK CENTRE AND ARENA
2500 CAMPEAU DR. • (613) 592-4282/4

JACK CHARRON ARENA
10 MCKITRICK DR. • (613) 592-4287

KANATA RECREATION COMPLEX
100 WALTER BAKER PL. • (613) 836-3121

NEPEAN
FOR THE LOCATIONS AND SCHEDULES OF NEPEAN'S OUTDOOR RINKS,
CALL (613) 727-6635.

BELL CENTENNIAL ARENA
50 CEDARVIEW RD. • (613) 828-9629

MERIVALE CENTENNIAL ARENA
1765 MERIVALE RD. • (613) 224-3168

NEPEAN SPORTSPLEX
1701 WOODROFFE AVE. • (613) 727-6683

WALTER BAKER SPORTS CENTRE
100 MALVERN DR. • (613) 825-2460

NEPEAN CIVIC SQUARE POND (OUTDOOR)
(613) 727-6700 EXT. 7615

OTTAWA
FOR THE LOCATIONS AND SCHEDULES OF OTTAWA'S OUTDOOR RINKS,
CALL (613) 244-5678.

BARBARA ANN SCOTT ARENA
PINECREST RECREATION COMPLEX
2240 TORQUAY AVE. • (613) 828-3118

BELLTOWN DOME
2915 HAUGHTON AVE. • (613) 828-3118

BREWER ARENA
210 HOPEWELL AVE. • (613) 247-4938

CANTERBURY ARENA
2185 ARCH ST. • (613) 247-4865

J. ALPH DULUDE ARENA
941 CLYDE AVE. • (613) 798-8246

JIM DURRELL RECREATION CENTRE
1265 WALKLEY RD. • (613) 247-4811

MCNABB ARENA
180 PERCY ST. • (613) 564-1070

SANDY HILL ARENA
60 MANN AVE. • (613) 564-1062

ST-LAURENT COMPLEX
525 CÔTÉ ST. • (613) 742-6767

TOM BROWN ARENA
141 BAYVIEW RD. • (613) 798-8945

RIDEAU TOWNSHIP
5572 DOCTOR LEACH DR., MANOTICK • (613) 692-4772

ROCKLAND
CORNER OF LAURIER ST. AND SIMONEAU ST. • (613) 446-6144/6022

VANIER
BERNARD-GRANDMAÎTRE ARENA
309 MCARTHUR AVE. • (613) 747-2528

WEST CARLETON TOWNSHIP
W. ERSKINE JOHNSTON ARENA
3832 CARP RD., CARP • (613) 839-3000

Game, Set and Match Rallying at PUBLIC TENNIS COURTS

F amilies that play together, stay together, right? Tennis is an affordable way to achieve this maxim. Whether you're practising or playing a serious match, an hour or two on the court serves up a healthy dose of summer exercise and fun. The City of Ottawa and other municipalities in the Capital Region maintain outdoor public courts to be used on a first-come, first-served basis. In addition, some communities have public tennis clubs where you don't have to be a member to book a court and play (call ahead for prices and times). While the range of facilities may vary, most municipal courts and public clubs offer instruction to players of every level. Your local school board may also offer lessons and playing time during the summer months.

CHELSEA
DUNNDEROSA GOLF & TENNIS CLUB
11, CH. NOTCH • (819) 827-1349

GLOUCESTER
BLACKBURN HAMLET TENNIS CLUB
2669 INNES RD. • (613) 824-0002

ORLÉANS TENNIS CLUB
1257 JOSEPH DROUIN AVE. • (613) 837-2845

HULL
SPORTHÈQUE DE HULL (INDOOR COURTS)
72, RUE JEAN-PROULX • (819) 777-5656

HULL HAS 24 OUTDOOR COURTS FOR ITS RESIDENTS. NON-RESIDENTS WHO PURCHASE A PASS (AVAILABLE FOR THE SEASON OR THE DAY) MAY ALSO USE THE COURTS. FOR MORE INFORMATION, CALL (819) 595-7400.

KANATA
MARCH TENNIS CLUB
2500 CAMPEAU DR. • (613) 592-6269

THUNDERBIRD GOLF & ATHLETIC CLUB
1927 RICHARDSON SIDE RD. • (613) 836-4150

NEPEAN
CRYSTAL BEACH TENNIS CLUB
71 CORKSTOWN RD. • (613) 721-2231

VALLEYSTREAM TENNIS CLUB
3412 RICHMOND RD. • (613) 828-7622

OTTAWA
THE CITY OF OTTAWA maintains 91 tennis courts at 46 sites that can be used
for 30 minutes on a first-come, first-served basis (residents have priority).
For more information call, (613) 244-5300 ext. 4007.

ELMDALE TENNIS CLUB
184 HOLLAND AVE. • (613) 729-3644

OTTAWA NEW EDINBURGH CLUB
504 ROCKCLIFFE WAY • (613) 746-8540

WEST OTTAWA TENNIS CLUB
300 GREENVIEW AVE. • (613) 828-7622

CHAPTER 4

PLACES TO PLAY

I f it were left up to kids, they'd play all day long. Fortunately for them, Ottawa-Hull is full of parks, amusement centres and other affordable destinations where children's fun is the number-one priority all year long. At Storyland, visitors come face-to-face with their favourite nursery rhymes. At Mont Cascades Water Park, thrill-seekers can't get enough of the water slides. There are also places to go indoor rock climbing, white-water rafting and go-carting. This chapter will also tell you where to find the best tobogganing runs and swimming beaches.

For parents who are looking to do something extra-special for their child's birthday this year, read on to discover which sites have accommodations for children's parties. Then make your plans. Whole days of fun await you.

Surf's Up at SPLASH WAVE POOL

2040 OGILVIE RD.
GLOUCESTER
(613) 748-4222

Splash Wave Pool, an indoor aquatic centre, offers something for everyone in the family. When the surf's up, older children will want to frolic in the wave pool, where breakers reach a metre high, or take turns riding the 34-metre long water slide. Their younger siblings may prefer the beach area in front of the wave pool, with its gentle slope to deeper water. Toddlers do best at Kiddy Cove. This warm-water wading pool features toys, water sprays and a colourful array of pint-sized slides that will amuse your little ones for hours. For adults, there is a lane pool for swimming lengths and a whirlpool.

A small outdoor playground is open during the summer and is accessible from inside the centre. It has sprays and sprinklers

☞ **SEASONS AND TIMES**
➛ Year-round. For a complete schedule of activities, call (613) 748-4222.

☞ **COST**
➛ Adults $5.90, children (1 to 18) $4.10.
Credit cards accepted.

☞ **GETTING THERE**
➛ By car, take Wellington St. east to County Rd. 174 E. (formerly Hwy. 17B). At Ogilvie Rd. turn south and watch for signs on your left. About 15 minutes from Parliament Hill. Free parking on site.

☞ **NEARBY**
➛ Gloucester Municipal Library, McDonald's™ Playland (Bethamy Woods Plaza).

☞ **COMMENT**
➛ Operated by the Municipality of Gloucester. Baseball fields and a mountain-bike track are behind the pool.

and a rubberized surface that is very forgiving to little knees and toes. A shallow stream, chock-full of water wheels and dams designed to be operated by children, follows a serpentine course through the playground.

There are well-maintained changing rooms for men, women and families, and the centre is staffed by qualified lifeguards. Splash Wave Pool also has facilities for children's birthday parties and offers swimming and life-saving instruction, aquafitness programs and aquatic camps.

Spring-loaded Action
LE CENTRE DE TRAMPOLINES BOING
(BOING Trampoline Centre)

550, BOUL. DE LA GAPPE (GAPPE BLVD.)
GATINEAU, QUÉBEC
(819) 246-2022

If your kids love to jump—on their beds, on chairs, on the antique sofa in your living room—take them to Le centre de trampolines BOING, where their bouncing will be encouraged. The centre offers lessons, given by a certified coach, that teach the basics of trampoline jumping. Children six and up are welcome to try out for the centre's competitive team each September—there are various levels of competition available. Weekly and monthly conditioning programs are open to athletes wanting to

☞ **SEASONS AND TIMES**
➤ Year-round: Daily, 9 am—11 pm (reservations required).

☞ **COST**
➤ Varies with the package.
Introductory course (12 sessions) $86.94.
Free time: $5 an hour.
Membership card (11 sessions): $43.47.

☞ **COMMENT**
➤ Only authorized individuals are permitted to perform difficult jumps.

enhance their performance in snow boarding or diving or other sports. The centre also has free-time hours when visitors can practise their moves at their own pace. Birthday parties are available and include an animator, music and a party room.

Tag! You're Hit!
LASER TAG AND
CAPTURE THE FLAG

Anyone with fond memories of playing tag as a youngster will remember the disappointment of games that ended when a player disputed being tagged it. In today's hi-tech version there are no close calls. Players use laser guns to "tag" their opponents and score points electronically. Groups of kids (and grown-ups) can play laser tag and its derivations at several establishments around town. While the facilities may vary between locations, the rules of the game—which usually lasts 20 or 30 minutes—are essentially the same: Opposing teams try to outscore each other while travelling through hostile territory.

Cyberdome

20-1200 ST. LAURENT BLVD. (ST. LAURENT SHOPPING CENTRE)
OTTAWA
(613) 742-6540
WWW.CYBERDOME.CA

☞ **SEASONS AND TIMES**
→ Year-round: Mon—Thu, 10 am—11 pm; Fri—Sat, 10 am—midnight; Sun, 11 am—10 pm.

☞ **COST**
→ Prices range between $0.50 and $7.

After a hard-fought game of Laserforce™ laser tag, combatants can unwind at some of the over 200 arcade games and virtual reality and motion simulators found here. Birthday parties are available.

Deep Space Laser

2680 QUEENSVIEW DR.
OTTAWA
(613) 820-2020

☞ **SEASONS AND TIMES**
→ Year-round: Mon—Thu, 4 pm—9 pm; Fri, 4 pm—11 pm; Sat, 11 am—11 pm; Sun, noon—6 pm.

☞ **COST**
→ $7 per person per game. During school breaks and on PD days, it's $5 per person after the second game. Free for non-playing escorts.

This is your chance to play a video game . . . from the inside. Shoot aliens and starships as you dodge down corridors in this spacious, multilevel playing area. Kids seven and under must be escorted by an adult. Birthdays and sleepovers can be arranged.

Laser Quest

1800 ST. LAURENT BLVD.
OTTAWA
(613) 526-4000

T here's ample room for hiding and seeking in this three-level maze. Though players of all ages are welcome, the management recommends not bringing children under seven. Video games are located in the lobby. Party rooms and birthday packages are available.

☞ **SEASONS AND TIMES**
➤ Summer, school breaks and holidays: Mon—Thu, 2 pm—10 pm; Fri—Sat, 2 pm—11 pm; Sun, noon—6 pm. Winter: Mon—Tue, reserved groups only; Wed—Thu, 6 pm—10 pm; Fri, 4 pm—11 pm; Sat, noon—11 pm; Sun, noon—6 pm.

☞ **COST**
➤ $7 per person per game.

Combat 307 Paint Ball

3415 UPLANDS DR.
OTTAWA
(613) 737-5019

C apture the Flag and its variations are played on a 49-hectare wooded site, so expect a game to last a few hours. Play is restricted to individuals ages 10 and over. Children under 15 must be accompanied by an adult.

☞ **SEASONS AND TIMES**
➤ Spring—fall (barring snow cover): Daily, 8 am—3 pm. Groups already on the premises may continue playing after 3 pm.

☞ **COST**
➤ $30 per person, including equipment rental, 100 rounds of paint balls and lunch. Extra ammunition can be purchased.

Indoor Rock Climbing

Most kids have an inborn love of climbing. Why not satisfy their desire to get higher with a visit to an indoor centre that has rock climbing facilities? You'll find qualified staff ready to instruct your children in proper climbing techniques on routes that have been designed to accommodate climbers of every ability. Safety equipment is provided and supervisory personnel are always on hand. Children as young as five are welcome. Climbing is an excellent exercise that builds body strength and the ability to concentrate—so adults should give it a try too!

Aztec Ascent Indoor Rock Climbing Centre

499 INDUSTRIAL AVE.
OTTAWA
(613) 739-1581

☞ **SEASONS AND TIMES**
➤ Year-round: Mon—Fri, 1 pm—midnight; Sat—Sun, 1 pm—9 pm.

☞ **COST**
➤ Climbing $ 10, shoe rental $ 3, harness rental $ 2.

Aztec has a $35 introductory package for beginners that includes a one-week membership, lessons and equipment rental. There are over 50 climbing routes on a 550-square-metre surface. Although individuals of all ages can participate, people holding the ropes (belaying) must be at least 12 years old. Birthday party packages are available.

Cyberdome Virtual Reality Theme Parks Inc.

20-1200 ST. LAURENT BLVD.
(ST. LAURENT SHOPPING CENTRE)
OTTAWA
(613) 742-6540

☞ **SEASONS AND TIMES**
➤ Year-round: Mon—Thu, 10 am—11 pm; Fri—Sat, 10 am—midnight; Sun, 11 am—10 pm.

☞ **COST**
➤ $5 per climb including equipment rental

C limbers ages five and up can use one of three paths (beginner, intermediate and advanced) to scale a wall nearly five storeys high. For a description of other activities offered at Cyberdome, see the entry under Laser Tag (page 86) in this chapter.

Running Wild in INDOOR GYMS

D o your children have energy to burn? Take them to an indoor adventure gym where slides, climbing nets, tunnels and pedal cars are made-to-measure for kids. Even though well-trained staff are on hand, children must be accompanied by an adult. Some centres offer organized activities, for example, arts and crafts, excursions and day camps. Most rent spaces for special occasions such as birthday parties.

☞ **NOTE:**
➤ Children are required to wear socks at all times.

Cosmic Adventures

1373 OGILVIE RD. • GLOUCESTER • (613) 742-8989

T he premises are non-smoking, peanut-free and accessible to wheelchairs. There is a café.

☞ Year-round: Daily, 9 am—8:30 pm. Reduced hours around Christmas. Call to confirm that they're open.
☞ Mon—Thu, children 4 and older $6.99, 2 to 3 years $3.99, 12 to 23 months $1.99, under 11 months free; Fri—Sun, add $1 to all prices.

Gym Jam

1642 MERIVALE RD. (MERIVALE MALL) • NEPEAN • (613) 723-7529

☞ Year-round: Mon and Thu, 9:30 am—8 pm; Tue—Wed, 9:30 am—6 pm; Fri—Sat, 9:30 am—9 pm; Sun, noon—6 pm. Reduced hours around Christmas. Call to confirm that they're open.
☞ Adults free, children 2 to 12 years $6.99, under 24 months $4.99 (youth 13 to 17 not permitted).

Gym-Max

105, BELLEHUMEUR • GATINEAU • (819) 246-0496

☞ Year-round: Daily, 24 hours.
☞ 3-month pass $120, 6-month pass $200, annual pass $300.

Midway Family Fun Park

2370 LANCASTER RD. • OTTAWA • (613) 526-0343

M idway's facilities now include a play centre for toddlers. While they're keeping busy at the slides and tunnels, their older siblings can ride the bumper cars or play mini-golf, bowling, basketball and video games.

☞ Year-round: Sun—Thu, 9 am—midnight; Fri—Sat, 9 am—1 am.
☞ Admission is free.
☞ Games: One to four tokens ($0.25 each).

Making a Splash at MONT CASCADES WATER PARK

MONT CASCADES RD.
CANTLEY, QUÉBEC
(819) 827-0301 OR **1-888-282-2722**
CASCADES@ISTAR.CA
WWW.MONTCASCADES.CA

A recent trend among popular ski resorts has been to provide summertime activities for off-season visitors. With the creation of its six-slide water park, Mont Cascades has joined the trend with a splash.

Small children will prefer Minisplash, which has a wading pool, a kiddy-size slide and water sprays. Minisplash is attended by lifeguards and restricted to kids under 121 centimetres. Older children will test their mettle on Black Magic, an exciting tunnel ride. For the brave of heart (and those over 132 centimetres) the Kamikaze provides an exhilarating six-storey plunge. Larger slides, such as Space River and Mammoth River, permit up to four people to descend together in a raft.

All the water slides are in full sun, so sun block is a must. The park has a restaurant or you can bring a

---

☞ **SEASONS AND TIMES**

➤ Summer: June 5—Sept 6, daily, from 10 am. Call ahead for closing times.
Winter: Dec—late Mar, daily, Mon, 10 am—9 pm; Tue—Fri, 10 am—10 pm; Sat, 9 am—9 pm; Sun, 9 am—5 pm.

☞ **COST**

➤ Water slides: Adults $15, students (9 to 15) $12.50, children (3 to 8) $10, under 2 free. Pool use only, $10. Reduced rates after 2 pm and 4 pm. Credit cards accepted.
Skiing (day and night): Adults $20.65, students $19.50, children (7 to 12) $18.35, under 6 free.

picnic and eat at the shaded picnic tables scattered throughout the site (no alcohol or glass containers are permitted). Though small, the changing areas are adequately maintained and lockers are available.

In the winter, Mont Cascades offers day and night skiing on 12 runs, snow boarding, ski lessons and equipment rentals.

☞ **GETTING THERE**

➤ By car, take Rideau St. east to King Edward Ave. Go north and cross the Macdonald-Cartier Bridge. From Autoroute 5 N. take Exit 5 (St. Joseph Blvd. N.) to Rte. 307 N. and continue to Mont Cascades Rd. There are posted signs. Drive carefully as the grades are very steep near the mountain. Free parking on site. About 25 minutes from Parliament Hill.

☞ **NEARBY**

➤ Rapides-Farmers Power Station; Ferme des 2 mondes, Cantley.

☞ **COMMENT**

➤ Privately run. The picnic areas and pool sides are accessible to wheelchairs. Plan a 3-hour visit.

☞ **SIMILAR ATTRACTIONS**

➤ **Walter Baker Sports Centre,** 100 Malvern Dr., Nepean, Ontario (613) 825-2468.
➤ **Logos Land Resort,** Cobden (about 90 minutes west of Ottawa). Water slides, beach, pedal boats, hiking trails and more. RR 1, Hwy. 17, Cobden, Ontario (613) 646-9765 or 1-877-816-6605.
➤ **Poplar Grove Trailer Park,** Hwy. 31 north of Greely, Ontario (613) 821-2973. Campground, mini-golf.

Thrills and Chills at the GREAT CANADIAN BUNGEE FAMILY AREA

MORRISON'S QUARRY
RTE. 105 N.
WAKEFIELD, QUÉBEC
(819) 459-3714 (GENERAL INFORMATION) OR **(819) 459-2676** (FAMILY AREA)
BUNGEE@MAGI.COM
HTTP://INFOWEB.MAGI.COM/~BUNGEE/

A ttention all thrill-seekers. North America's highest bungee jump is located right here at Great Canadian Bungee. But you don't have

---

☞ SEASONS AND TIMES

➤ Spring: May—June, weekends, 11 am—6 pm.
Summer: July—Aug, Mon—Fri, 3 pm—6 pm; weekends, 11 am—6 pm.
Fall: Sept—Oct, weekends, 11 am—6 pm.

☞ COST

➤ Site admission: Adults $4, children $2 (includes kayaks and pedal boats).
Bungee jump: Starting at $67.60 for students (minimum weight 37 kilograms), 5 or more $59 (reservation required), 20 or more $49 (reservation required).
Cable slide: $29.90.

☞ GETTING THERE

➤ By car, take Rideau St. east to King Edward Ave. and go north across the Macdonald-Cartier Bridge. Continue on Autoroute 5 N. to Rte. 105 and take it north to the quarry. It's just south of Wakefield. Free parking on site. About 25 minutes from Parliament Hill.

☞ COMMENT

➤ Privately operated. The lake water is not government tested. Plan to spend the day.

to jump to enjoy a visit to this abandoned limestone quarry. For most people, watching others take the leap from the 20-storey cliff is excitement enough.

Tamer adventures include riding the cable slide or kayaking on the lake. In fact, Great Canadian Bungee offers a clean and attractive setting for family outings or birthday parties. There is a sandy beach, a supervised swimming area, pedal boats, a spacious picnicking site, playing fields and changing rooms. Scuba divers may be interested in exploring the old airplane that's found its final resting place at the bottom of the lake.

Life in the Fast Lane at KIDDY KARS ZOO

1979 Labonté
Clarence Creek
(613) 488-2650

Rev up your kids with a visit to Kiddy Kars Zoo, where they can take a spin on a paved circular track in a battery-operated go-cart. There are about 25 vehicles to choose from including cars, trucks, Jeeps and scooters. Designed for children ages 2 to 10, the go-carts have a weight limit of 40 kilograms, which means older children and

☞ **Seasons and Times**
→ May–Oct, daily, 9:30 am–8 pm (weather permitting).

☞ **Cost**
→ Go-carts: $7 per hour per child. Petting zoo and play area included.

parents have to sit this one out. Safety headgear is not provided.

There are other attractions here too. A sandy play area has slides and swings, and a petting zoo houses chickens, cows and other barnyard animals. For climbing fun, your children will enjoy the playhouses and miniature castle. Kiddy Kars Zoo holds children's sleepovers (bring a tent and sleeping bag). Birthday parties can be arranged.

☞ **GETTING THERE**

➤ By car, take Wellington St. east (its name changes to Rideau St., then Montreal Rd.) and get on County Rd. 174 E. (formerly Hwy. 17 E.), which becomes County Rd. 17 E. Access County Rd. 8 S. (Landry Rd.) and follow the Kiddy Kars Zoo signs to Clarence Creek. Turn west on Labonté and drive to the village outskirts. It's on the left. Free parking on site. About 40 minutes from Parliament Hill.

☞ **SIMILAR ATTRACTIONS**

➤ **Kiddy Kars**, 963 Limoges Rd., Limoges (613) 443-0726.
➤ **Kiddy Kars**, 2356 Mer Bleue Rd., Orléans (613) 837-4727.
➤ **Kiddy Kars**, 5200 Flewellyn Rd., Kanata (613) 599-8663.

Stepping through the Looking Glass at STORYLAND FAMILY PARK

STORYLAND RD., R.R.#5
RENFREW
(613) 432-2222 OR 1-800-205-3695
(613 AND 819 AREA CODES ONLY)

A family favourite, Storyland has enchanted children for more than three decades with its 30 animated scenes of classic nursery rhymes. To find them, follow the earthen trails. Each scene has a bilingual text to be read aloud. Then press the button. Your children will watch with delight as the story is illuminated and figurine characters move about to music.

There are lots of fun things to do at the park. Kids will love bouncing on the giant inflated trampoline (it's supervised) or touring the frog and turtle pond in a pedal boat. The playground has tunnel slides, swings and more. Visitors can also play mini-

☞ **SEASONS AND TIMES**
➙ June 6—Sept 7, daily, 9:30 am—6 pm.

☞ **COST**
➙ Adults $8.50, seniors and students (5 to 15) $7.90, children (2 to 4) $6.90, under 2 free.
Additional fee to use the pedal boats. Half price after 4 pm. Credit cards accepted.

☞ **GETTING THERE**
➙ By car, take O'Connor St. south to Hwy. 417 W. and access Hwy. 17 N. Take the Storyland Rd. Exit (about 10 kilometres past Renfrew) and turn north. Look for Storyland on your left after a few minutes. Be careful turning into the parking lot the oncoming traffic is hard to see. Free parking on site. About one hour from Parliament Hill.

golf or ride in non-motor-
ized go-carts. Bring swimsuits so your kids can play
games under the sprin-
klers. If you want to pack a
picnic, the park has tables

☞ **COMMENT**
►Visitors can remain on the grounds
and enjoy the story scenes after closing. Bring insect repellent. Plan a
half-day visit.

---

located in clean and spacious eating areas near the main
entrance and beside the playground.

Sing Along with KARAOKE

For an evening of unbridled fun take your whole family to a karaoke bar or restau-rant, where everyone can get into the act. Enthu-siasm is all that counts. Kids especially seem un-concerned with their stage

---

☞ **COST**
► Usually included with the price of
the meal.

☞ **COMMENT**
► The variety of English music is
usually good, though the selection of
French tunes can be limited.

---

presence or ability to sing on key. All they want to
know is if their favourite songs are available. The
Karaoke Hot-line—(613) 745-7337—tracks events
around town and may be able to suggest a venue that's
right for you. Or ask at your local family restaurant for
their schedule of karaoke afternoons and evenings.
Here are the names of two places to get you started . . .

Rock Around the Clock

161 MONTREAL RD.
OTTAWA
(613) 744-6861

Kids' karaoke is Sunday afternoons between 2 pm and 6 pm.

Virgin's Restaurant

2660 SOUTHVALE CRES.
OTTAWA
(613) 737-7378

Virgin's offers karaoke seven nights a week and claims to have the biggest karaoke library in Ottawa, including a large selection of French-Canadian songs. If you're not ready to face a big audience come early in the evening and avoid Friday and Saturday nights.

Rafting on the OTTAWA AND ROUGE RIVERS

For the ride of your life try white-water rafting. Several outdoor adventure companies offer half-day and day-long rafting tours (lunches included) for families. Different tours are available: gentle excursions suitable for children as young as seven (minimum 23 kilograms) and more exhilarating rides for kids 12 years and up (minimum

4.1 kilograms). Experienced guides are in the driver's seat. Most rafting companies offer other outdoor activities such as canoeing, kayaking and camping.

ESPRIT RAFTING
CH. THOMAS LEFEBVRE
DAVIDSON, QUÉBEC
(819) 683-3241 OR 1-800-596-7238
WWW.ESPRITRAFTING.COM

NEW WORLD RIVER EXPEDITIONS
100, CH. RIVIÈRE ROUGE
CALUMET, QUÉBEC
(819) 242-7238 (INFORMATION) OR 1-800-361-5033 (RESERVATIONS)

OWL RAFTING
FORESTERS FALLS, ONTARIO
(613) 646-2263 OR 1-800-461-7238
WWW.OWL-MKC.CA

RIVER RUN RAFTING & PADDLING CENTRE
BEACHBURG, ONTARIO
(613) 646-2501 OR 1-800-267-8504
WWW.RIVERRUNNERS.COM

WILDERNESS TOURS WHITEWATER RAFTING
BEACHBURG, ONTARIO
(613) 646-2291 OR 1-800-267-9166
WWW.WILDERNESSTOURS.COM

☞ **SEASONS AND TIMES**
➤ Apr—Oct, daily (depending on weather and water conditions).

☞ **COST**
➤ Though costs vary, expect to pay at least $35 per person. Prices generally include equipment rental, a professional guide and a picnic lunch. Reservations are required.

Puttering Around at MINI-GOLF

T hirty minutes and a good sense of humour are all it takes to play 18 holes of mini-golf. While the principle is the same as regular golf—sink the ball in the hole using the fewest strokes—this scaled-down version puts obstacles in the way of

☞ **SEASONS AND TIMES**
➤ May—Oct, daily during mid-summer, weekends only at the start and end of the season. 10 am—dusk, usually.

☞ **COST**
➤ Varies, but generally: Adults $6.50, children $4.50.

you and your target. The better the course, the better the obstacles, which may include tunnels, bridges, water, windmills and silhouettes of popular cartoon characters. Most kids love the challenge, but some will be frustrated by a game that looks easier than it is. Balls, putters and scorecards are supplied, though it's up to you whether you keep score or not. After playing a round head to the "clubhouse" for an ice cream or other refreshment. Some mini-golfs host children's birthday parties.

GATINEAU DRIVING RANGE AND MAXI-PUTT
255, CH. EDEY, AYLMER • (819) 682-2960

EMBRUN GOLF CLUB INC.
1483 NOTRE DAME, EMBRUN • (613) 443-4653

MINI PUTT L'AUTHENTIQUE
205, BOUL. DE LA GAPPE, GATINEAU • (819) 561-0427

INNES ROAD GOLFLAND
CORNER OF INNES RD. AND PAGE RD., GLOUCESTER • (613) 824-6580

TARGET GOLF CENTRE
4870 BANK ST., GLOUCESTER • (613) 822-9141

MINI GOLF LE TROPICAL
975, BOUL. ST-JOSEPH, HULL• (819) 776-1216

OPTI-PUTT
198, RUE MONTCALM, HULL • (819) 776-4091

WACKYPUTT/LE RIGOLFEUR
1040, BOUL. ST-JOSEPH, HULL • (819) 775-3050

DOUBLE DECK GOLF CENTRE
1565 MAPLE GROVE RD., KANATA • (613) 591-0006

STAN'S PUTT PUTT LAND
1905 RICHARDSON SIDE RD., KANATA • (613) 831-3848

ON THE GREEN DRIVING RANGE & MINI GOLF
5510 LIMEBANK RD., MANOTICK • (613) 822-2616

MINI GOLF GARDENS
2 COLONNADE RD. N., NEPEAN • (613) 723-5359

ORLÉANS GOLF CENTRE
2127 MER BLEUE RD., ORLÉANS • (613) 837-7746

AIRPORT GOLFLAND
3600 PAUL ANKA DR., OTTAWA • (613) 521-0890

THUNDERBIRD GOLF & GO-KARTS
3145 CONROY RD., OTTAWA • (613) 739-3064
THEY ALSO HAVE VOLLEYBALL AND ARCADES.

KARTERS' KORNER
6336 FALLOWFIELD RD., STITTSVILLE • (613) 831-2828
THEY ALSO HAVE GO-CARTS, VOLLEYBALL AND ARCADES.

Take a Break at McDONALD'S™ PLAYLANDS

D id you know your kids are welcome at McDonald's™ play areas even if you don't buy a meal from the restaurant? A godsend during bad weather, these indoor parks feature tunnel slides, carousels and rooms filled with plastic balls. Though the layout varies from outlet to outlet, several tables in each restaurant juxtapose the glassed-in area, permitting parents to sip a quiet coffee while watching the kids. Should you decide to purchase food, children can order a kid-size meal that comes with a toy. Disposable bibs and highchairs are available and the place mats can be coloured, so bring crayons. Birthday parties can be arranged.

2000 MONTREAL RD. • (BETHAMY WOODS PLAZA), GLOUCESTER • (613) 741-8578
515, BOUL. ST-JOSEPH, HULL • (819) 770-2296
126 ROBERTSON RD., NEPEAN (BELL'S CORNERS) • (613) 829-2803
3773 STRANDHERD DR., NEPEAN • (613) 823-7838
2643 ST. JOSEPH BLVD., ORLÉANS • (613) 837-2866
2380 BANK ST., OTTAWA • (613) 526-1258

Sandy Swimming
BEACHES

Nothing beats the summer heat like a swim at the beach. The Ottawa-Hull area, blessed with many rivers and lakes, has lots of excellent swimming beaches that are ideal spots for family outings. At the following sites, the water is clean and there's plenty of fine sand for toddlers to dig in. Not all of these beaches offer supervised swimming, and some have modest user fees. Changing facilities, toilets and concession stands are usually found nearby. Watercraft can be rented at some locations.

AYLMER MARINA
Rte. 148 W.
Aylmer, Québec
(819) 684-5372

BAXTER CONSERVATION AREA
Dilworth Rd. (five kilometres south of Kars)
Kars
(613) 489-3592

CITY OF OTTAWA
Beach information: (613) 244-5678

BRITANNIA BAY
Richmond Rd. to Britannia Rd. on the Ottawa River.

MOONEY'S BAY
Riverside Dr. on the Rideau River.

WESTBORO BEACH
Ottawa River Pkwy. (west of the Champlain Bridge).

GATINEAU, QUÉBEC
LAC BEAUCHAMP
Lac Beauchamp Park
745, boul. Maloney
(819) 669-2548

GATINEAU PARK
Beach information: (819) 827-2020

MEECH LAKE (O'Brien and Blanchet beaches)
Exit 12 off Autoroute 5 N.

LAC LA PÊCHE
Eardley Rd. off Rte. 366 W.

LAC PHILIPPE (Breton and Parent beaches)
Lac Philippe Pkwy. off Rte. 366 W.

FITZROY PROVINCIAL PARK
Canon Smith Rd.
Fitzroy Harbour
(613) 623-5159

HULL, QUÉBEC
LEAMY LAKE
Leamy Lake Park
Off Rte. 148 E.
(819) 239-5617

Great Tobogganing
HILLS

Everyone has stories about "the best" tobogganing hill. That's because everyone loves tobogganing, even those of us who have forgotten what it feels like to career down a snowy slope on a piece of wood or plastic that threatens to go out of control at any moment. The following is a listing of popular tobogganing runs in the Ottawa-Hull area. Take your kids, and this time don't just stand at the top of the hill . . . go for a ride yourself, just one more time.

CHELSEA, QUÉBEC
LARRIMAC
CH. LARRIMAC OFF RTE. 105 N.

GATINEAU, QUÉBEC
LAC BEAUCHAMP PARK
745, BOUL. MALONEY
(819) 669-2548

GLOUCESTER
CONROY PIT
NCC GREENBELT
SOUTH OF HUNT CLUB RD. (PARKING LOT #15)
LIGHTING UNTIL 11 PM.
(613) 259-5433

GREEN'S CREEK
NCC GREENBELT
BEARBROOK RD. (PARKING LOT #24)
LIGHTING UNTIL 11 PM.
(613) 259-5433

HULL, QUÉBEC
LES GLISSADES DU LAC DES FÉES
425, BOUL. GAMELIN
(819) 777-3337
TWELVE SLIDES, LIFT, INNER TUBES, GROOMED HILLS, LIGHTED.

KANATA

BRIDLEWOOD PARK
OFF BRIDLEWOOD DR.
KANATA RECREATION COMPLEX
100 WALTER BAKER PL.

NEPEAN

CEDARVIEW ROAD SAND PITS (PARKING LOT #12)
NGC GREENBELT
OFF CEDARVIEW RD.
(613) 259-5433

OTTAWA

CARLINGTON PARK
941 CLYDE AVE.

CHAPEL HILL
SUNNYSIDE AVE. NEAR BANK ST.

DOMINION ARBORETUM
EXPERIMENTAL FARM
EXPERIMENTAL FARM DR. AT PRINCE OF WALES DR.

MOONEY'S BAY PARK
OFF RIVERSIDE DR. (BETWEEN WALKLEY RD. AND BROOKFIELD RD.)

VINCENT MASSEY PARK
OFF HERON RD. (BETWEEN RIVERSIDE DR. AND COLONEL BY DR.)

CHAPTER 5

PLACES TO LEARN

P art of the fun of parenting is satisfying your children's endless curiosity about the world around them. There are many sites in the Ottawa-Hull area that will help you do this in a fun way. This chapter includes locations where kids can experience a simulated earthquake, watch money being minted, help out at a fish farm, visit a hydro-electric dam, explore a cavern deep underground and learn about forest ecology. Shhh! Just don't tell them these outings are educational.

Shaking All Over at
THE ÉCOMUSÉE
DE HULL

170, RUE MONTCALM (MONTCALM ST.)
HULL, QUÉBEC
(819) 595-7790
ECOMUSEE@VILLE.HULL.QC.CA
HTTP://ECOMUSEE.VILLE.HULL.QC.CA

A nyone who has wondered what an earthquake feels like can find out here. Children and adults alike will head for the Earthquake Room, where a high-tech simulator re-creates tremors of up to six on the Richter scale.

Situated beside Brewery Creek near a picturesque waterfall, this attractive indoor museum, though small, houses several displays. Learn about the Earth's evolution and some of our more pressing environmental issues. Study the display of minerals and crystals on the huge interactive map, then test your knowledge of geology. Visit the fossil

☞ **SEASONS AND TIMES**
➤ Summer: May 1—Sept 1, daily, 10 am—6 pm.
Winter: Oct 1—Apr 30, Tue—Sun, 10 am—4 pm.

☞ **COST**
➤ Adults (16 and older) $5, students, seniors and children $4, under 6 free, families $10.

☞ **GETTING THERE**
➤ By car, take O'Connor St. south to Albert St. and turn west (it runs into Wellington St., but continue straight). At Booth St. turn north and cross the Chaudières Bridge. Follow Eddy St. to Papineau, turn west and continue to the end. The Écomusée is at the corner, on Montcalm St. Free parking on site. About 10 minutes from Parliament Hill.
➤ By public transit, take OC Transpo bus 8 to Hull (Alexandré-Taché Blvd. and Montcalm St.) and transfer to STO bus 21 or 35. OC Transpo tickets aren't accepted on STO buses. Pay again, or walk 10 minutes from the bus stop to the museum. For information, call OC Transpo (613) 741-4390 or STO (819) 770-3242.
➤ By bicycle, follow the car directions.

☞ **COMMENT**

➤ Guided tours are only offered to groups with reservations. Plan a 45-minute visit.

exhibit or take in the extensive insect collection or the life-size replica of a dinosaur. The museum also features a pictorial exhibit that traces Hull's development, and hands-on displays to teach users how public utility services operate. An attendant is on hand to answer your questions.

A Spelunker's Delight
LAFLÈCHE CAVES

818 CH. BLACKBURN (BLACKBURN RD.)
VAL-DES-MONTS, QUÉBEC
(819) 457-4033 OR 1-877-457-4033

Y our kids probably don't know what spelunking is. Take them on a 75-minute tour of Laflèche Caves and they'll find out soon enough. They'll get to put on a hard hat complete with headlamp and descend below the surface of the earth into a gigantic cavern. At 402 metres long, these caves are among the largest in the Canadian Shield. Visitors of all ages are fascinated by the sinkholes, the giant stalactites, the long twisting corridors and the slumbering colonies of bats that are found inside. Experienced guides provide commentary about the cave's history.

☞ **SEASONS AND TIMES**

➤ Year-round: Daily (reservations mandatory).

☞ **COST**

➤ Mon–Thu, adults $8, students $6, children (5 to 12) $4; Fri–Sun, adults $12, students $8, children (5 to 12) $6.

Wear warm clothes as the cave varies between 3°C and 7°C year-round. Unlike other caves, this one is fairly dry so you won't need a change of clothing for afterward. Good walking boots are essential. If you have younger children (normally kids must be at least five to go on the tours, though exceptions can be made), tell them what to expect before coming so

☞ **GETTING THERE**
➤ By car, take Wellington St. east (its name changes to Rideau St.) to King Edward Ave. Go north over the Macdonald-Cartier Bridge and access Autoroute 50 E. Take Exit 138 (Archambault Blvd.) to Rte. 307 and go north, following the signs to the caves. Free parking on site. About 45 minutes from Parliament Hill.

☞ **SIMILAR ATTRACTIONS**
➤ **Bonnechere Caves**, Eganville (613) 628-2002.
➤ **Lusk Cave, Gatineau Park** (819) 827-2020 or 1-800-465-1867.

they won't get frightened underground. There is a lunchroom that has vending machines, or bring a picnic. Birthday parties and workshops can be arranged.

Seeing How Electricity Is Made at
THE RAPIDES-FARMERS POWER STATION

Rte. 307 N. (av. Principale Ave.)
Gatineau, Québec
1-800-365-5229

There are three hydro-electric stations on the Gatineau River, but only Rapides-Farmers is open for visits. Five 75-minute guided tours are given daily to separate groups of English and French-speaking visitors. Although the educational aspect of the visit will likely be lost on smaller children, they should still enjoy the spectacular sights and sounds of an electric station in operation.

After watching a 15-minute video in the welcome centre that discusses electricity and safety, everyone is given a hard hat to wear. Then you will proceed on foot into the very bowels of the dam. This is where the electricity is generated, and you had better be prepared for the din. The area is filled with giant spinning turbines, and the water that feeds them plunges almost 20 metres here. Each tour also includes a visit outside to the top of the dam, where a second station, Chelsea, is visible upstream. Afterward, you may return to the welcome centre and view poster displays about the uses of electricity in everyday life.

☞ SEASONS AND TIMES

➤ Guided tours in summer only.

May 17—June 23, Mon—Fri, 9 am, 10:30 am, 12 pm, 1:30 pm, 3 pm.

June 24—Labour Day, Wed—Sun, 9:30 am, 11 am, 12:30 pm, 2 pm, 3:30 pm.

☞ COST

➤ Free.

☞ GETTING THERE

➤ By car, take Wellington St. east (its name changes to Rideau St.) to King Edward Ave. and go north. Cross the Macdonald-Cartier Bridge and follow Autoroute 5 N. Take Exit 5 to Rte. 105 N. toward Cantley (follow the signs for Mont Cascades) and cross the Gatineau River. At Principale Ave. turn west and continue to the dam. Poorly indicated, it's easy to spot next to the road. Free parking on site. About 15 minutes from Parliament Hill.

➤ By bike, take the Alexandra Bridge north to the Voyageurs Pathway immediately after the bridge. Go east through Jacques Cartier Park. At Leamy Lake Park, access Fournier Blvd. E. and cross the bridge to Gatineau. At St-Jean-Baptiste turn north (it becomes Principale Ave.) and continue to the dam. About 10 kilometres from Parliament Hill.

☞ COMMENT

➤ Operated by Hydro-Québec.

☞ SIMILAR ATTRACTIONS

➤ **Carillon Dam (Hydro-Québec)**

Guided tours in summer only.

Victoria Day—June 24, Mon—Fri, 9 am, 10:30 am, 12 pm, 1:30 pm, 3 pm.

June 25—Labour Day, Wed—Sun, 9:30 am, 11 am, 12:30 pm, 2 pm, 3:30 pm.

Groups of 10 or more need to reserve in advance.

On Hwy. 344 W. It's near Lachute, east of Hawkesbury 1-800-365-5229.

➤ **R. Moses-R. Saunders Dam** (between Cornwall and Massena, New York). Rte. 131 N., Massena, New York (315) 764-0226.

Fishing for Fun and Facts at THE OUTAOUAIS FISH FARM

2104 CLARK RD.
ROCKLAND
(613) 446-5057

This farm offers a wide range of fun activities for children ages 4 to 13. But at the heart of the visit is learning how rainbow trout are raised. Each four-hour tour includes time in the hatchery, demonstrations of daily chores, a video and educational games. The children will also see how trout develop from tiny eggs into five-kilogram adults. Other exhibits have live displays of common Ontario fish, including smallmouth bass and pike.

The fun really gets going when the children are invited to feed the ravenous trout—always a crowd pleaser—or to try their luck in the trout ponds. Rods and bait are supplied by the hatchery, however, $3.50 is charged for each fish that is landed. Staff is on hand to clean and wrap the catch. The ponds are open to the public on weekends.

The farm also runs a dynamic forest ecology program for children. During the half-day tour they will go on a nature walk to identify trees and

---

☞ **SEASONS AND TIMES**

➤ Fish program (for groups only):
Apr—Oct, by reservation.
Forest ecology program (for groups only): Apr—Oct, by reservation.
Public fishing: May—June, Mon—Fri, 2:30 pm—5 pm; weekends, 10 am—6 pm.
July—Aug, daily, 10 am—6 pm.

☞ **COST**

➤ Fish and forest ecology programs:
$6 a person per program.
Weekend fishing: $3.50 per fish caught.
Cash only.

plants, visit a beaver dam, do nature crafts and participate in a treasure hunt.

☞ **GETTING THERE**
➤ By car, take Wellington St. east (its name charges to Rideau St.) to County Rd. 174 (formerly Hwy. 17 E.), which becomes County Rd. 17. Just past Rockland, take Rte. 8 S. (Landry Rd.) and follow the signs. Free parking on site. About 35 minutes from Parliament Hill.

☞ **NEARBY**
➤ Kiddy Kars, Papanack Park Zoo, Cumberland Heritage Village Museum.

☞ **COMMENT**
➤ Only the trout ponds are wheelchair accessible. No fishing permit required. Bilingual service.

An Education in Trees
McKINNON FORESTRY CENTRE

18655 KENYON RD.
APPLE HILL
(613) 528-4430
WWW.VISIT.CORNWALL.ON.CA

Kids will learn a lot about forest ecology here. A good place to start is the Conference Centre, which has taxidermal displays of forest wildlife. Logging tools and forest management

☞ **SEASONS AND TIMES**
→ Summer: July–Aug, Sun–Thu,
9 am–3 pm.
Other seasons: Sun and Mon, 9 am–
3 pm, or by appointment.

☞ **COST**
→ Free. Fees apply for some activities.

☞ **GETTING THERE**
→ By car, take Wellington St. east (its name changes to Rideau St., then Montreal Rd.) to Aviation Pkwy. and turn south. Merge onto Hwy. 417 E. and take Exit 58 (Hwy. 138 S.) to the town of Monkland. Access County Rd. 43 E. to County Rd. 20 and go south past Apple Hill. Turn east on Kenyon Rd. and drive about two kilometres to the centre. It's on the left. Free parking on site. About one hour from Parliament Hill.

☞ **NEARBY**
→ Nor'Westers and Loyalists Museum.

☞ **COMMENT**
→ Sponsored by Domtar. The buildings are accessible to wheelchairs, the trails are not.

☞ **SIMILAR ATTRACTION**
→ **MacSkimming Outdoor Education Centre.** Courses and programs for all ages, including nature studies, skiing, orienteering, canoeing and outdoor survival skills. 3635 County Rd. 174 (formerly Hwy. 17), Cumberland (613) 833-2080.

exhibits, complete with explanatory panels, can be found in the Museum Building nearby. With this introduction under your belt, it's time for a nature walk. Five kilometres of woodland paths wind through the centre. Take along a brochure to help you identify the trees, which include oak, pine and birch. And don't forget the mosquito repellent!

In addition to offering a range of nature programs, the centre has workshops and outdoor activities such as nighttime excursions to find owls and hikes that involve identifying edible plants. Bilingual educational programs are offered to schools and there is a summer camp for 8 to 12-year-olds. You can also attend seasonal events, including the Forest Fest (early October), which features a lumberjack competition. Call for details or check out the centre's Web site.

Basking in Bullion at THE ROYAL CANADIAN MINT

320 SUSSEX DR.
OTTAWA
(613) 993-8990 OR 1-800-276-7714
WWW.RCMINT.CA

The minute you step through the doors of the Royal Canadian Mint you'll stop taking coins for granted. During the 45-minute guided tour you'll watch how coins are transformed from designs on paper into the gleaming end product. Although the tours are geared toward adults, even children will be intrigued by the process. But you won't find pennies or quarters being produced here. Coinage for everyday use is made in Winnipeg. This mint designs and fabricates commemorative coins for Canada and other nations, including Ghana and the Philippines.

The tour includes a history of Canadian money and information on the

☞ **SEASONS AND TIMES**
➤ Year-round: Daily, 9 am—5 pm.

☞ **COST**
➤ Individuals 6 and over $2, under 6 free, families $8. Group rates available.

☞ **GETTING THERE**
➤ By car, take Wellington St. east to Sussex Dr. and go north to Guigues St. Pay parking at the National Gallery of Canada. The mint is three blocks north. Minutes from Parliament Hill.
➤ By public transit, take OC Transpo buses 3 or 306.
➤ By bicycle or foot, follow the car directions. It's about a 10-minute walk.

☞ **NEARBY**
➤ Canadian War Museum, Parliament Hill, Ottawa Locks, Bytown Museum, National Gallery of Canada, Major's Hill Park, Peacekeeping Monument.

☞ **COMMENT**
➤ Despite the "reservations only" notices, group tours are given every 15 minutes in summer

mint's origins, which began operations in 1907. You'll also have the chance to visit a vault and see a million dollars in solid gold. Afterward you can browse at the boutique, where commemorative coins and jewellery are on sale. The Royal Canadian Mint also has an interesting Web site with teaching modules geared to kids ages 5 to 15 that explain the fundamentals of coin minting.

Learning about Geology at
LOGAN HALL

601 Booth St. and Hwy. 17B
Ottawa
(613) 995-4261
LFRIEDAY@NRCAN.GC.CA

Though small, this museum is a haven for anyone with an interest in rocks. It was named for Sir William Logan, the founder of the Geological Survey of Canada, and showcases a sampling of the survey's immense collection of rocks, minerals, gems, fossils, meteorites and ores from across Canada and around the world.

You will find exhibits about Sir Logan and other leading Canadian geologists, interactive geological maps and videos to teach you about the survey's research projects. Perhaps one of the best presentations focusses on the history of geology in Canada and

> ☞ **SEASONS AND TIMES**
> ➤ Year-round: Mon—Fri, 8 am—4 pm.
>
> ☞ **COST**
> ➤ Free.

features the 570-million-year-old fossil Sir Logan found in Québec's Gaspé region in 1859. Its discovery fueled the debate between creationists and evolutionists over Darwin's treatise on evolution, which was published the same year.

The museum is well suited for school-age children who are curious about geology, but younger children will fidget. A bookstore devoted to geology is located off the foyer.

☞ **GETTING THERE**

➤ By car, take Wellington St. west to Booth St. and turn south. After crossing Gladstone St., watch for the Geological Survey of Canada building—the museum is inside. One-hour street parking. Minutes from Parliament Hill.
➤ By public transit, take OC Transpo buses 14 or 316.
➤ By bicycle, take the Gladstone bike route to Booth St. and turn south. Bicycle parking on site.

☞ **COMMENT**

➤ Operated by the Geological Survey of Canada. Plan a 45-minute visit.

Making a Side Trip to the
ST. ALBERT CHEESE FACTORY

150 ST. PAUL ST.
ST. ALBERT
(613) 987-2872

I f you're planning a day of strawberry or apple picking at Cannamore Orchards, you'd do well to visit the nearby dairy in St. Albert. Located about 10 kilometres southeast of Crysler, St. Albert Cheese Factory has been in operation for nearly 100

years. Tours are no longer given, but the dairy has a delicatessen on site where you can sample and purchase a variety of freshly made foods, including cheddar, havarti, ice cream and frozen yogurt. The deli also sells fixings for picnic lunches, which you can enjoy at the well-maintained, sheltered picnic area.

Groups can watch a video that demonstrates how the cheese is made (call one week in advance to arrange a weekday viewing). Copies of the video are also available for lending (a refundable security deposit is required).

Mid-August is a good time to visit the dairy as that's when it holds its annual Cheese Festival. The four-day event features bingo, karaoke, performances by country singers, clowns and magicians and cheese tasting, naturally.

CHAPTER 6

MUSIC, THEATRE DANCE & CINEMA

When we think of "culture vultures," we usually think of adults. But take your children to a play or concert at the National Arts Centre or to an open-air show at Odyssey Theatre and you'll see that the love of the arts knows no age. Many theatres and cultural centres around town have regular presentations of music, variety, drama and dance that never fail to enchant younger audiences. This chapter contains a rundown of the venues that stage productions appropriate for kids. You'll also find an idea or two for places where children can receive instruction in the performing arts, including acting and clowning. For movie buffs with a penchant for non-Hollywood films, we've provided the names of film festivals and repertory movie houses offering cinema for kids or families.

Seeing the Big Picture
IMAX™ FILMS

(At the Canadian Museum of Civilization)
100, rue Laurier (Laurier St.) Hull, Québec
(819) 776-7010 (information), (819) 776-7014 (groups),
(613) 755-1111 (tickets) or (819) 776-7018 CINÉPLUS (rental)

You haven't enjoyed a big-screen experience until you've sat through a movie at an IMAX™ theatre. Its seven-storey projection screen places every audience member at the centre of the action. Whether you're watching a feature on the pyramids or a documentary following climbers up Mount Everest, when the film begins you'll be glued to your seat. The CINÉPLUS theatre at the Canadian Museum of Civilization (page 30) has regular showings in English and French of IMAX™ and OMNIMAX™ films (the latter are viewed on a dome-shaped screen in a hall equipped with surround sound). Tickets can be purchased from Ticket Master or at the museum box office. New and popular movies sell out quickly, so buy your tickets early. Groups of 200 or more can arrange to rent one of the cinemas for a private screening (a $1,500 cost at time of printing).

☞ Seasons and Times

➛ Year-round: Call for show times.

☞ Cost

➛ $5.50 to $8 depending on the program.

☞ Getting There

➛ By car, take Wellington St. east to Mackenzie Ave. and go north across the Alexandra Bridge to Laurier St. and turn west. The museum is on the left. Pay parking on site ($8 maximum). Free street parking on Sundays (arrive early). Minutes from Parliament Hill.

➛ By public transit, take OC Transpo bus 8 (Albert St.).

➛ By bicycle or foot, use the car directions. It's about a 30-minute walk.

Shows for Kids at THE NATIONAL ARTS CENTRE

53 ELGIN ST.
OTTAWA
(613) 996-5051 (INFORMATION)
OR (613) 755-1111 (TICKETS)
HTTP://WWW.NAC-CNA.CA

D
on't put off taking your family to the National Arts Centre (NAC), where your children will thrill to performances of music, theatre and dance. Among the offerings for kids are concert series (Young Peoples Concerts, Student Matinées), plays, musicals and appearances by popular children's entertainers. Both the National Arts Centre Orchestra and Festival Canada—a summertime extravaganza of theatre, music and cabaret—are based at the NAC, which also hosts such galas as the Ottawa International Jazz Festival and Dance Canada. For behind-the-scenes entertainment, take a one-hour guided tour (twice daily in summer) of the NAC's dressing rooms and other backstage areas. Groups should call (613) 996-5051 ext. 665. Opera Lyra offers school groups the chance to attend an open dress rehearsal two days before each opera opens. Call (613) 233-9200 for information.

☞ **SEASONS AND TIMES**
➤ Performances: Year-round. Call for information about upcoming children's shows.
Backstage tours: Late June—early Sept, daily, 11 am and 2 pm.

☞ **COST**
➤ Performances: Call for information.
Backstage tours: Individuals $2, families (one or two adults with children) $5.

If your kids have a yen to take centre stage, the NAC, in conjunction with the Ottawa School of Speech & Drama, runs the Young Actor's Space. This series of theatre workshops covers everything from clowning to melodrama for students in grades 2 to 13. To register, call (613) 567-6788.

☞ **GETTING THERE**
➤ By car, take Wellington St. east to Elgin St. and go south. The NAC is on the east side of Elgin in Confederation Park. Underground pay parking is available. Minutes from Parliament Hill.
➤ By public transit, take OC Transpo buses 5, 6, 14, 16 or 18.
➤ By bicycle or foot, use the car directions.

☞ **NEARBY**
➤ National War Memorial, Ottawa Art Gallery, Parliament Hill, Confederation Park.

Theatre under the Stars at STRATHCONA PARK

ODYSSEY THEATRE
OFFICES: 2 DALY AVE. (ARTS COURT)
PERFORMANCES: STRATHCONA PARK
LAURIER AVE. E. AND RANGE RD.
OTTAWA
(613) 232-8407

O dyssey Theatre has been delighting Ottawa-Hull families every summer for over a decade with open-air productions at Strathcona Park. Working in the Italian street-theatre tra-

---

☞ **SEASONS AND TIMES**
➤ July 22–Aug 22, Tue–Sun, 8:30 pm; Wed matinée, 1 pm; Sun matinée, 2 pm.

☞ **COST**
➤ Adults $20, students and seniors $17, children under 12 $8. Groups (10 or more): $17 each. Meet the actors: $4 per person. Sunday matinée: Pay what you can.

☞ **GETTING THERE**

→ By car, take Elgin St. south to Laurier Ave. and turn east. Continue to Range Rd. Free parking on site. Minutes from downtown.

→ By public transit, take OC Transpo bus 5.

→ By bicycle or foot, follow the car directions. It's about a 30-minute walk.

☞ **NEARBY**

→ Laurier House.

dition of Commedia dell'arte, the company blends music, myth, masks and movement to create magical theatrical experiences. The one-hour matinée on Wednesdays, which is a shorter version of the show, is ideal for youngsters. After the Wednesday matinée, by prior arrangement, groups can meet the actors and get a closer look at the masks and costumes. There are tables in the park and a children's playground. Bleachers provide seating for audiences, or bring a lawn chair. A blanket will come in handy as it can get chilly in the evening.

More Theatre for Kids

There's a slew of theatres and theatrical companies in the National Capital Region that offer entertainment for families at reasonable prices. For information about current and upcoming productions, call:

Centre culturel l'Auberge Symmes

1, RUE FRONT • AYLMER • (819) 685-5033

Music, plays, films and expositions, including performances specifically designed for children. In French.

Centrepointe Theatre

101 CENTREPOINTE DR. • NEPEAN • (613) 727-6650
HTTP://WWW.CITY.NEPEAN.ON.CA/THINGS/THEATRE

While most of their productions are aimed at families, those in the Family Fair Subscription Series are definitely for kids. In English.

Cumberland Town Hall Theatre

255 CENTRUM BLVD. • ORLÉANS
(613) 741-7170 (INFORMATION) OR (613) 837-0381 (TICKETS)

Children will love their Dreamweaver Children's Series and Cookies & Art program. In English.

MIFO

CENTRE CULTUREL D'ORLÉANS
6600 CARRIÈRE ST. • ORLÉANS • (613) 830-6436

In addition to its La Série Jeunesse for children, the MIFO has a variety of other plays, some of which are suitable for families. In French.

Ron Maslin Playhouse/Kanata Theatre

1 RON MASLIN WAY • KANATA • (613) 831-4435
HTTP://KT.OTTAWA.COM/KT1.HTML

This amateur company stages several plays each year, including one designed for children. In English.

Salamander Theatre

2 DALY AVE. (ARTS COURT) • OTTAWA • (613) 569-5629

I n addition to touring schools with their plays, Salamander has theatre classes and summer camps for young thespians. In English.

Salle Jean-Despréz, Maison du Citoyen

25, RUE LAURIER • HULL • (819) 595-7411

A variety of shows aimed at a family audience are mounted every year. In French.

Théâtre de l'Île

1, RUE WELLINGTON • HULL • (819) 595-7455

S everal amateur and professional companies are based here. Some productions may interest children. There is also a summer dinner theatre. In French.

Living in CINÉ

I f you don't much care for the films coming out of Hollywood these days, you're in luck. Alternative films are increasingly available. NFB videos, repertory cinemas and film festivals offer enter-tainment that's suitable for everyone at an afford-able cost.

National Film Board

T he National Film Board (NFB) is well known for the quality and originality of its productions, which include numerous children's films and ani-mated shorts. Many NFB movies are available on video and can be borrowed from these libraries.

CARLETON UNIVERSITY LIBRARY
1125 COLONEL BY DR. • (613) 520-2735

Students, faculty and staff at Carleton and other Ontario universities may borrow materials. Annual memberships are available to the general public for $75 ($25 for Carleton alumni).

While videos are not available through inter-library loan, you can get a NFB membership at these libraries so it won't cost to borrow NFB material (it doesn't confer other borrowing privileges).

GLOUCESTER PUBLIC LIBRARY
(ORLÉANS BRANCH)
1705 ORLÉANS BLVD.
(613) 824-1962

NEPEAN PUBLIC LIBRARY
(CENTRAL BRANCH)
101 CENTREPOINTE DR.
(613) 727-6649

OTTAWA PUBLIC LIBRARY
(MAIN BRANCH)
120 METCALFE ST.
(613) 236-0301

Repertory Houses

Watching movies on the big screen doesn't have to squeeze your pocketbook. Repertory cinemas may not show the big-name films as soon as first-run theatres do, but you can't argue with their prices, which are even lower when you purchase a membership. One or two-month schedules are available, so you can plan ahead for your night, or nights, out at the movies.

BYTOWNE CINEMA
325 RIDEAU ST. • OTTAWA • (613) 789-3456

Runs a variety of recent kids' movies during March break.

☞ Admission (March break): $3 per person. Other times: Adults (non-members) $8, (members) $5, seniors and children 12 and under $4. Memberships: $8 a year.

MAYFAIR REPERTORY CINEMA
1074 BANK ST. • OTTAWA • (613) 730-3403

Family matinées some weekends.

☞ Adults (non-members) $7.50, (members) $5.50, seniors and children 13 and under $4. Memberships $15 a year, includes 3 free admissions.

Film Festivals

OTTAWA INTERNATIONAL ANIMATION FESTIVAL

NATIONAL ARTS CENTRE/WORLD EXCHANGE CINEMA
OTTAWA
(613) 232-6315
HTTP://WWW.AWN.COM/OTTAWA

Many of the films shown during the Ottawa International Animation Festival, held between late September and early October, are suitable for children. Keep an eye out for Children's Day, which is popular with kids. They get to watch films made by their peers, tour an animation studio and produce their own movie. Participants must register. For details, call (613) 232-8769.

☞ Individual tickets: Adults $8, seniors and children under 12 $5. Children's Day: $25.

THE STUDENT ANIMATION FESTIVAL OF OTTAWA (SAFO)

2 DALY AVE., SUITE 120
OTTAWA
(613) 232-8769
HTTP://WWW.AWN.COM/SAFO

Kids can attend the film premieres of student productions and first-time animators at this festival. The four-day competition, which is held in late October at the National Archives of Canada Auditorium, has categories for high school students and animators under 12.

CANADIAN CHILDREN'S MUSEUM FILM FESTIVAL

100, RUE LAURIER (LAURIER ST.)
CANADIAN MUSEUM OF CIVILIZATION, HULL
(819) 776-8282

The films presented at this festival, made by children ages 9 to 18, are in competition for honours. Though the public screenings are held at the museum in November, the filmmakers must enter their short films and videos months ahead (the deadline for submissions is April 15). Juried submissions are sent to compete at the National Children's Film Festival in Indianapolis. For more information about competition entries, contact Lynn McMaster at the Canadian Children's Museum or by e-mail at lynn.mcmaster@civilization.ca.

Community
CENTRES

Families with an interest in the arts should check out their local community centre. Chances are it presents movies, concerts, dance and theatre productions and art expositions throughout the year. Many of the performances are just right for children. Even better, the admission is minimal or free. Most centres publish schedules of upcoming shows and events, or look for one at your library, in the local paper or in the calendar of events distributed by most municipalities to their residents each spring and fall.

CHAPTER 7

Animals,
Farms
& ZOOS

O ttawa is inextricably linked to its rural roots, which is good news for folks who enjoy getaways to the country. Whether your family hankers to pick apples off a tree or eat maple taffy off the snow, the region surrounding Ottawa-Hull is the place to go. This chapter provides a rundown of destinations that will take you out of the city to feed cuddly animals at Valleyview Little Animal Farm or ride horseback at Pinto Valley Ranch. For a taste of the more exotic, visit Papanack Park Zoo or the Reptile Rainforest. There are also outings to Bearbrook Farm, the Wild Bird Care Centre, the RCMP Stables and the National Capital Equestrian Park, which offers instruction in riding. So make your plans, pack up your van and head out for a day of family fun.

Helping the Zoo Keepers at
PAPANACK PARK ZOO

150 NINE MILE RD.
WENDOVER
(613) 673-7275

Feeding time will be the highlight of your visit to Papanack Park Zoo, as that's when your children will be invited to help with the animals. They might be asked to hold a three-metre-long python or toss apples across a fence to black bears.

Originally an animal refuge and breeding centre, today the zoo is open to the public. With over 100 native and exotic creatures living in the farmlike setting, there is lots to see. Follow the grassy and earthen trails to find cougars, wolves, foxes, tigers, reptiles and many other creatures. Attend the daily feline-feeding demonstration or let your youngsters be photographed with animals at the Meet the Keepers event.

Children ages 10 and up may be interested in attending the summer

☞ **SEASONS AND TIMES**
➤ Summer: Victoria Day weekend—June, daily, 11 am—4 pm; July—Aug, daily, 10 am—5 pm; Sept—Thanksgiving, daily, 11 am—4 pm. Winter. Dec, weekends, 11 am—3 pm; Christmas—New Year's and March break, daily, 11 am—3 pm.

☞ **COST**
➤ Adults $7, youth (12 to 18) $5, older children (6 to 11) $4, small children (2 to 5) $3, under 2 free. Admission to the reptile house is extra. Memberships available. Some credit cards accepted.

☞ **GETTING THERE**
➤ By car, take Wellington St. east (its name changes to Rideau St., then Montreal Rd.) to County Rd. 174 (formerly Hwy. 17 E.), which becomes County Rd. 17. At Wendover look for Nine Mile Rd. (Rte. 19). Turn south and follow the signs to the zoo. Free parking on site. About 40 minutes from Parliament Hill.

☞ **NEARBY**
→ Outaouais Fish Farm, MMF
Pheasants, Kiddy Kars, Alfred Bog Walk.

☞ **COMMENT**
→ Small-wheeled strollers are hard
to push on the rough paths. Plan a 4-
hour visit.

zoo-keeper day camp. They'll learn how to prepare animal feed, look after the young and perform a variety of tasks related to animal care. Papanack also has summer facilities for children's birthday parties. In winter, bilingual staff will entertain young party guests in your home with reptiles from the park. Children can visit Santa at the zoo in December.

❧ ❧ ❧

All Creatures Great and Small
VALLEYVIEW LITTLE ANIMAL FARM

4750 FALLOWFIELD RD. (WEST OF MOODIE DR.)
NEPEAN
(613) 591-1126
WWW.CAPCAN.CA

☞ **SEASONS AND TIMES**
→ Spring: Tue—Fri, 10 am—3 pm;
weekends and holidays, 10 am—
4 pm. Open for March break.
Summer: July 1—Labour Day, Tues—
Sun, 10 am—5 pm.
Fall: Labour Day—Oct 31, Tue—Fri,
10 am—3 pm; weekends and holidays, 10 am—4 pm.

A nimals and more animals, that's what you'll find at this farm. Visit the Little Red Barn to see pigs, ducks, chickens and their barnyard buddies. (If you really want to make friends, buy some feed for the animals at the main gate beforehand.) Were your kids expecting more exotic creatures? Then take them on the Country Walk to find yaks, llamas and ostriches, to name a few. Leave time for a ride on the Funny Farm Express wagon train or for a puppet show at the Century-Old Red Barn. Or head over to the playground called Tweety Town.

The farm offers a range of daily activities—all you have to do is check the schedule at the Little Red Barn. Also, there are seasonal events for families, including maple syrup and pancake parties, corn roasts and harvest festivals.

☞ **COST**
➤ $4.25 per person.

☞ **GETTING THERE**
➤ By car, take O'Connor St. south to Hwy. 417 W. and access Hwy. 416 S. Take Exit 66 and go west on Fallowfield Rd. Just past the grain silos, turn south. Free parking on site. About 20 minutes from Parliament Hill.

☞ **NEARBY**
➤ Stony Swamp Conservation Area, The Log Farm, Wild Bird Care Centre, Lorenzetti Park, Saunders Farm.

☞ **COMMENT**
➤ The tap water isn't potable—bring your own or get it from the restaurant. Plan a 4-hour visit.

Horsing Around at the ROYAL CANADIAN MOUNTED POLICE STABLES

CANADIAN POLICE COLLEGE
ST. LAURENT BLVD. AND SANDRIDGE RD.
OTTAWA
(613) 993-3751
HTTP://WWW.RCMP-GRC.GC.CA

Long recognized for excellence in horseman-ship, the RCMP has been performing the Musical Ride to thrilled audiences for over a century. Did you know your family could visit the sta-bles of this famous team of horses and their riders? At the end of your guided half-hour tour you'll know the names of the horses, their heights and how old they are. You'll also know why the RCMP's horses are black—to highlight the riders' red tunics.

Visitors are invited to inspect the riding equip-ment and to ask questions of staff. If you're lucky, you might see team members putting the horses through their paces in the training arena. If the team is on tour, which is usually between June and September, other RCMP horses will be stabled in their place. At the open house in

---

☞ **SEASONS AND TIMES**

➤ Stable tours: Year-round, week-days, 8:30 am—10:30 am and 12:30 pm—3:30 pm; Oct—Apr, until 3 pm.
Open house: Usually the first Saturday in December, 10 am—3 pm. Call for details.
Canadian Sunset Ceremony: Generally the last weekend in May.

☞ **COST**

➤ Tours: Free.
Open house: Donation of non-per-ishable foods.

December you can visit the stables, take in a police dog demonstration, view RCMP displays or go for a wagon ride (the program varies each year). The Musical Ride is performed during the Canadian Sunset Ceremony on the college's grounds in late May.

☞ **GETTING THERE**
➤ By car, take Wellington St. east to St. Laurent Blvd. and turn north. St. Laurent ends at the Canadian Police College where the stables are located. Free parking on site. About 10 minutes from Parliament Hill.
➤ By public transit, take OC Transpo bus 7.

☞ **NEARBY**
➤ National Aviation Museum, Rideau Hall, Rockcliffe Park, Rideau Falls Park.

☞ **COMMENT**
➤ Operated by the RCMP. Plan a 1-hour visit.

Sitting Tall in the Saddle at
PINTO VALLEY RANCH

1969 GALETTA RD.
FITZROY HARBOUR
(613) 623-3439

C owpokes of every ability will enjoy riding the trails at this western-style ranch. With over 100 horses to choose from, experienced riders and novices alike will be certain to find the right mount. Children 11 years old and younger can ride on ponies in the rodeo corral, where an attendant is on hand. For horsemen 12 and up, the range is much larger. Pinto Valley offers individuals or groups guided rides by the hour or day along four trails that wind through 24 hectares of woods and fields.

The ranch also features buggy and wagon rides, a petting zoo and special events such as western jamboree parties and a June rodeo. Winter fun includes sleigh rides followed by bean suppers, tobogganing, cross-country skiing and skating on the ranch's pond. Pinto Valley has facilities for receptions, picnics and children's birthday parties.

☞ **SEASONS AND TIMES**
➤ Summer: May–Sept, daily, 9 am–9 pm.
Winter: Oct–Apr, daily, 9 am–dusk. Closed Christmas Day.

☞ **COST**
➤ Pony ring: $10 per half hour.
Horseback riding: $20 per hour.
Daily and group rates available. Cash only.

☞ **GETTING THERE**
➤ By car, take O'Connor St. south to Hwy. 417 W. and access Hwy. 17 N. Take the March Rd. N. exit to Dunrobin Rd. and go north. At Galetta Rd. drive west and follow the signs to the Quyon ferry. The ranch is on your right just before the ferry landing. Free parking on site. About 30 minutes from Parliament Hill.

☞ **NEARBY**
➤ Fitzroy Provincial Park.

☞ **COMMENT**
➤ Bicycle helmets are supplied to riders or they may wear their own safety headgear.

☞ **SIMILAR ATTRACTIONS**
- **Bean Town Ranch**, 2891 Concession 3, Plantagenet, Ontario (613) 860-7433.
- **Captiva Farms**, ch. de la Montagne, Wakefield, Québec (819) 459-2769.
- **Double D Ranch**, County Rd. 17 (formerly Hwy. 17 E.), Cumberland, Ontario (613) 833-2317.
- **Happy Trails Riding Stables**, 5979 Leitrim Rd., Carlsbad Springs (613) 822-1482.
- **Sundance Ranch**, County Rd. 8, east of Manotick, Ontario (613) 692-3052.

Making Tracks to the WILD BIRD CARE CENTRE

734 MOODIE DR.
NEPEAN
(613) 828-2849
WILDBIRD@CYBERUS.CA
WILDBIRD.CYBERUS.CA

Foster your children's love of wildlife by taking them to see the birds at this avian hospital, which has answered tens of thousands of calls to assist injured birds since opening its doors in the early 1980s. After nursing them back to health, the staff returns the birds to the wild. Visitors can tour the centre and see turkey vultures, owls, crows, songbirds and many other species that are recuperating in the aviaries. Most of the residents are

☞ **SEASONS AND TIMES**
- Year-round: Daily, noon—3 pm. Closed Christmas and New Year's days.

☞ **COST**
- Free (donations are requested).

☞ **GETTING THERE**
➔ By car, take O'Connor St. south and follow the signs to Hwy. 417 W. Access Hwy. 416 S. and take Exit 72 (Knoxdale/West Hunt Club). Go west on Knoxdale, then south on Moody Dr. Look for the centre where the power lines cross the road. Free parking at Stony Swamp Conservation Area lot P8. About 20 minutes from Parliament Hill.

☞ **NEARBY**

➔ Stony Swamp Conservation Area.

☞ **SIMILAR ATTRACTION**

➔ **Cushing Lodge Raptor Centre.** Raises and releases such endangered species as golden eagles, falcons, vultures and owls. Visitors can see the birds and learn about them. Ladysmith, Québec (819) 647-3226. cushing@istar.ca

☞ **COMMENT**

➔ Plan a 30-minute visit.

indigenous species, but there are a few exotic types as well, including a peacock. Your kids can meet Mojo the crow, the centre's mascot, and they'll delight in the antics of the ducks that reside in a bathtub. If you want to see baby birds, the best time to visit is in May.

The centre is located in the Stony Swamp Conservation Area, so you might want to combine your visit with a few hours of hiking or snowshoeing. The Beaver, Chipmunk and Jack Pine trails are nearby, and there are picnic areas.

Taking Riding Lessons at the NATIONAL CAPITAL EQUESTRIAN PARK

401 CORKSTOWN RD.
NEPEAN
(613) 829-6925

Taking riding lessons is just the thing for children who have an interest in joining the horsy set. The National Capital Equestrian Park has private and group English riding instruction for individuals ages seven and older. Thanks to its spacious heated indoor arena, the centre offers lessons year-round. There are also riding day camps in the summer and during school breaks.

The Equestrian Park sits amidst 110 hectares of parkland and has five outdoor rings, a show jumping course and several riding trails. During the year, it's the site of competitions, including the Capital Classic Show Jumping Tournament in July, which attracts lots of families.

☞ **SEASONS AND TIMES**
➤ Year-round: Lessons by arrangement.

☞ **COST**
➤ Group lessons start at $90 for four one-hour sessions.

☞ **GETTING THERE**
➤ By car, take O'Connor St. south and follow the signs to Hwy. 417 W. Take Exit 134 (Moodie Dr.) and go north to Corkstown Rd. Free parking on site. About 15 minutes from Parliament Hill.
➤ By public transit, take OC Transpo bus 166. Tell the driver your destination. The bus stop is 500 metres from the Equestrian Park.

☞ **COMMENT**
➤ Operated by the City of Nepean Parks and Recreation Department.

Loitering with Lizards at the REPTILE RAINFOREST

152 PRESCOTT ST.
KEMPTVILLE
(613) 258-3529

☞ **SEASONS AND TIMES**
➤ Year-round: Tue—Sat, 11 am—
5 pm; Sun, 11 am—4 pm.

☞ **COST**
➤ Individuals $2.50, seniors $2,
children 2 and under free. Some
credit cards accepted.
Group tours: Call for details.
School visits: Starting at $100
(Mondays preferably).

☞ **GETTING THERE**
➤ By car, take O'Connor St. south and
follow the signs to Hwy. 417 W. Take
Exit 132, access Hwy. 416 S. and con-
tinue to Exit 34. Drive west on County
Rd. 43. At the first traffic light turn
south on Rideau St., then east on
Clothier St. (at the first stop sign), then
south on Prescott. Continue to the Red
& White store in Kemptville; Reptile
Rainforest is accessible from the park-
ing lot behind it. Free parking on site.
About 50 minutes from Parliament
Hill.

☞ **NEARBY**
➤ Baxter Conservation Area.

☞ **COMMENT**
➤ Plan a 1-hour visit.

If your children are fascinated by snakes, lizards and other scaly creatures, take them to the Reptile Rainforest, a small captive breeding centre that's home to nearly 100 species of reptiles, amphibians and spiders. You'll see boa constrictors, black water snakes, geckos, carnivorous African clawed frogs, bearded dragons and tarantulas, to name just a few of the animals on display. Some of them are endangered species. Kids can get an extra thrill by tossing food to the snapping turtles (a coin-operated feed machine is nearby). Visitors' self-guided tours are augmented by explanatory panels in front of each aquarium. There are also guided tours, reserved for school groups, that offer students the chance to touch the animals and learn about their biology. Reservations are required. Staff will also visit schools and bring some of the animals with them.

Getting Cozy with the Animals at BEARBROOK FARM

8411 Russell Rd.
Navan
(613) 835-2227 or **1-800-668-4477**
http://www.bbcanada.com/**144**.html

A trip to Bearbrook Farm should satisfy anyone with an interest in unusual animals. This game ranch is home to ostriches, elk, emus, deer, shaggy Highland cattle and wild boar. You'll also find sheep, turkeys, ducks and geese. Your kids will have fun feeding the livestock. (Animal feed can be purchased at Bearbrook's on-site grocery.) Afterward, youngsters can cuddle the rabbits, goats and other docile residents of the petting zoo.

The two-kilometre-long trail that leads to the animal pens is mostly unshaded, so bring your hats and sun screen. If you have small children who

☞ **SEASONS AND TIMES**
➹ Year-round: Daily, 9 am—5 pm. Visitors can remain on the grounds after closing time. Closed Christmas and New Year's days.

☞ **COST**
➹ Adults $8, children $3.50 (3 and up), babies free.
Credit and debit cards accepted.

☞ **GETTING THERE**
➤ By car, take O'Connor St. south to Hwy. 417 E. Continue to Exit 88 (Rockdale Rd.), turn north and follow the Bearbrook signs. At Rte. 26 (Russell Rd.), turn west and watch for the farm on your left. Free parking on site. About 25 minutes from Parliament Hill.

☞ **NEARBY**
➤ Cumberland Heritage Village Museum, Cannamore Orchard.

☞ **COMMENT**
➤ English, French and German service. Visitors can remain on the grounds after closing time. Plan a 2-hour visit.

tire easily, you may want to ride in a golf cart, which can be rented at a modest price. Bicycles are also welcome. The farm has a well-equipped playground and picnic facilities that include barbecues. The grocery sells drinks, deli goods and meat from the ranch. Bearbrook also operates a bed and breakfast and has a room for receptions and children's birthday parties.

Harvesting and Halloweening at CANNAMORE ORCHARD

RR #4
CRYSLER
(613) 448-3633 OR (613) 567-3000

Cannamore Orchard grows five popular apple varieties: McIntosh, Cortland, Spartan, Empire and Lobo. Visit between mid-August and Thanksgiving and pick your own apples or purchase pre-picked fruit by the bag. Grown on dwarf trees, the apples are easy to reach, even the ripest, reddest ones near the top. In-season strawberries and pumpkins are also for sale. When the fun turns to work, steer your children to the petting zoo or the pony rides, or take the whole family for a tour of the orchard in a horse-drawn wagon.

For a dose of the delightfully frightful, bring your kids to Cannamore just before Halloween. They'll love the Spooky Wagon Ride, the straw and cornstalk mazes and the haunted village, where actors are dressed up as witches and goblins.

Cannamore's gift shop sells pies, apple cider, jams, maple products and honey. The farm also holds children's birthday parties.

☞ SEASONS AND TIMES
➤ Mid-June—mid-July, daily, 7 am—7 pm.
Mid-Aug—Oct 31, Mon—Fri, 10 am—6 pm; weekends, 10 am—5 pm.

☞ COST
➤ Haunted Village, Spooky Wagon Ride: Adults (13 and older) $9, youth (5 to 12) $7, children under 5 free. Regular wagon rides: $1 per person. Fruit picking: No admission. While prices depend on crop conditions, expect to pay around $2 per kilogram for strawberries and $0.90 per kilogram for apples.

☞ GETTING THERE
➤ By car, take O'Connor St. south and access Hwy. 417 E. Take Exit 88 (Vars) and follow Rte. 17 S. There are posted signs to the orchard. Free parking on site. About 35 minutes from Parliament Hill.

☞ NEARBY
➤ St. Albert Cheese Factory, Hector Dignard et fils Blueberry Farm, Kiddy Kars (Limoges).

☞ COMMENT
➤ Family-owned. Plan a 3-hour visit.

☞ SIMILAR ATTRACTIONS
➤ These sites also have special activities at Halloween:
Proulx Sugar Bush and Berry Farm, 1865 O'Toole Rd., Cumberland (613) 833-2417.
Saunders Farm, 7893 Bleeks Rd., Munster (613) 838-5440. Other farms where you can pick your own fruit can be found on pages 148 and 149.

Bountiful Harvests
PLACES TO PICK APPLES

Apple-loving residents of the Ottawa-Hull area are fortunate to have a variety of orchards nearby that grow many different kinds of apples. Pack a picnic lunch and take your family on an apple-picking outing. Make sure to call ahead of time. Some orchards have no facilities, while others have gift shops, tractor rides, fresh produce for sale and toilets. Watch for orchards that advertise minimal spraying or *arrosage minimale*, which means they use pesticides sparingly.

Apple-picking season begins in late August and ends in late October, though dates may vary depending on the apple variety and that year's growing conditions. Expect to pay about $18 for a bushel basket. You can also visit the orchards in late May, when the blossoms are usually at their peak. The following orchards are within an hour's drive of Ottawa-Hull.

CANNAMORE ORCHARDS (PAGE 146)
RR #4 • EMBRUN • (613) 448-3633, (613) 567-3000

ORLEANS FRUIT FARM/FRUITS ORLÉANS
1399 ST. JOSEPH BLVD. • ORLÉANS • (613) 830-1303

MOUNTAIN ORCHARDS
10175 CLARK RD. • MOUNTAIN • (613) 989-5601

VERGERS DU RUISSEAU
235, CH. EARDLEY • AYLMER, QUÉBEC • (819) 682-0422

CUMBERLAND HERITAGE VILLAGE MUSEUM
2940 QUEEN ST. • CUMBERLAND • (613) 833-3059
THOUGH YOU CAN'T PICK APPLES HERE, THERE'S LOTS TO DO AT THE MUSEUM'S APPLEFEST ON THANKSGIVING DAY. ACTIVITIES INCLUDE CIDER MAKING, APPLE TASTING AND VISITING THE FARM ANIMALS.

The Sweet Taste of Summer
PLACES TO PICK STRAWBERRIES

Strawberries are never better than when eaten straight from the plant on a warm summer day. And that's what you get to do when you go strawberry picking. The season usually begins in the third week of June and lasts about a month, though some farms produce a second crop later in the summer.

The strawberry varieties grown in the Ottawa-Hull region are small, but they're bursting with flavour.

> ☞ **SEASONS AND TIMES**
> ➤ Late June—late July, daily, 10 am— 7 pm.
>
> ☞ **COST**
> ➤ Approximately $2 per kilogram. What you eat in the fields is free.
>
> ☞ **COMMENT**
> ₁ The Scottish names Fraser and Frazier are derived from the French word *fraisier*, which means strawberry farmer.

Luckily, there's no shortage of farms nearby where you can pick your own. Like apple orchards, however, the facilities at each farm vary between locations. Some have tractor rides and on-site restaurants, while others provide only baskets and fields of berries. Remember to bring sun hats for everyone as the fields are in full sun. These strawberry farms are within an hour of Ottawa-Hull.

CANNAMORE ORCHARDS (PAGE 146)
RR #4 • EMBRUN • (613) 448-3633 OR (613) 567-3000

DANIEL BÉLAIR
154, RUE PRUDHOMME • CANTLEY, QUÉBEC • (819) 827-0641
THEY ALSO HAVE RASPBERRIES AND SWEET CORN.

LES JARDINS CHARTRAND
356, CH. BOUCHER • AYLMER, QUÉBEC • (819) 684-6934
THEY ALSO SELL BEDDING-OUT PLANTS IN THE SPRING.

MOUNTAIN ORCHARDS
10175 CLARK RD. • MOUNTAIN • (613) 989-5601
THEY ALSO HAVE RASPBERRIES AND APPLES.

PROULX FARM
1865 O'TOOLE RD. • CUMBERLAND • (613) 833-2417

SAUNDERS FARM
7893 BLEEKS RD. • MUNSTER • (613) 838-5440 • WWW.SAUNDERSFARM.COM

A Taste of the Past
SUGAR BUSHES
(CABANES À SUCRE)

C ome late winter, when the sap starts to flow from Ontario and Québec's maple trees, families make their plans to attend sugaring-off parties. Highlighted by good food, much merriment and lots of maple syrup, the lively celebrations continue a tradition that is centuries old.

Native peoples from the Great Lakes and St. Lawrence regions were making maple syrup long before the Europeans arrived. Later, they showed French settlers how to tap the trees, collect the sap and reduce it to syrup. It's a laborious task—after hours of boiling, 40 litres of watery sap produce just one litre of syrup. The settlers also learned to celebrate the job's completion with a party. They square-danced, went for sleigh rides, prepared large banquets and poured steaming syrup onto the snow to make taffy.

Today, plastic piping and mechanized production have replaced the wooden buckets of yesteryear, but the celebration endures. This year, why not join in the festivities at one of these sugar bushes near Ottawa-Hull?

Bean Town Ranch
2891 Concession 3 • Plantagenet • (613) 860-7433
Seasonal activities year-round.

Cabane à Sucre Brazeau
316, Côte St-Charles • Papineauville, Québec • (819) 427-5611
Mar—Apr.

Cabane à Sucre Chez Ti-Mousse
442, Côte St-Charles • Sainte-Angélique, Québec • (819) 427-5413
Mar—Apr.

Cabane à Sucre Chez Vieille-Mère
349, Côte St-Charles • Papineauville, Québec • (819) 427-8241
Mar—Apr.

Charette Maple Farm
2681 County Rd. 17 (east of Rockland) • (613) 446-4939
Year-round.

Domaine de l'Ange-Gardien
1031-B, ch. Pierre-Laporte • Buckingham, Québec • (819) 281-0299
Mar—Apr.

Érablière de l'Outaouais
967, Mtée. McLaren • Gatineau, Québec • (819) 669-4969
Mar—Apr.

Fulton's Pancake House and Sugar Bush
291 6th Concession Rd. • Pakenham • (613) 256-3867 • www.fultonsfarm.com
Spring: Mar—Apr, daily, 9 am—5 pm.
Fall: Last weekend in Sept, first two weekends in Oct, 10 am—4 pm.

MacSkimming Outdoor Education Centre
3635 County Rd. 174 (formerly Hwy. 17) • Cumberland • (613) 833-2080
Year-round.

Proulx Farm
1865 O'Toole Rd. • Cumberland • (613) 833-2417
Seasonal activities year-round.

STANLEY'S OLDE MAPLE LANE FARM
2452 YORKS CORNERS RD. • METCALFE • (613) 821-2751
MAR—APR.

VALLEYVIEW LITTLE ANIMAL FARM
4750 FALLOWFIELD RD. • NEPEAN • (613) 591-1126
YEAR-ROUND.

WHEELERS PANCAKE HOUSE
AND MAPLE SUGAR CAMP
HIGHLAND LINE • MCDONALDS CORNERS, WEST OF LANARK VILLAGE
(613) 278-2788 • WWW.WHEELERSMAPLE.COM
SEASONAL ACTIVITIES YEAR-ROUND.

CHAPTER 8

green
spaces

Parks are natural destinations for family outings. Fortunately, Ottawa-Hull has many fine parks where you and your kids can picnic in the shade of old trees, kick around a ball, enjoy the scenery and generally get away from it all. But some parks provide opportunities of a more exciting variety. At Jacques-Cartier Park your kids can race down a snowy slide. At Fitzroy Provincial Park they can build sand castles on the beach. At the Mer Bleue Conservation Area they can explore a sphagnum bog. For a few days of canoe-camping, head to Gatineau Park, or to any of the other parks listed here where you can hike, cycle, snowshoe or cross-country ski. Parks allow you to create your own fun, and at the end of the day, that's what family outings are all about.

Untamed Wilderness
GATINEAU PARK

VISITOR CENTRE, 318 MEECH LAKE RD.
CHELSEA, QUÉBEC
(819) 827-2020 OR 1-800-465-1867
GPVISITO@NCC-CCN.CA
WWW.CAPCAN.CA

Located minutes from Ottawa, Gatineau Park is a popular destination for swimmers, campers, cyclists, skiers and wildlife enthusiasts. It boasts nearly 312 square kilometres of open spaces and wilderness, 125 kilometres of hiking trails (90 of which are open to mountain bikes) and several outstanding beaches. First-time visitors will want to drop by the Visitor Centre to pick up information about the park's facilities and to purchase trail maps for the summer ($3) and winter ($4.95).

If you're planning to stay only a few hours, head to the Parkway Sector, which is one of three sectors in the park and closest to town. In summer you can tour the Mackenzie King Estate (page 180), go swimming at Meech Lake, hike through woodlands along scenic trails or enjoy a picnic lunch at one of the many picnicking areas. For wilder surroundings, go to either the Lac Philippe

---

☞ **SEASONS AND TIMES**

➤ Visitor Centre:
Summer: Mid-May—early Sept,
daily, 9 am—6 pm.
Winter: Sept—mid-May, Mon—
Fri, 9:30 am—4:30 pm; weekends,
9 am—5 pm.

☞ **COST**

➤ Parkway Sector:
Access: Free. Swimming and Mackenzie King Estate, $6 per person.
Lac Philippe and Lac La Pêche sectors:
Access: $6 per vehicle.
Camping: Call (819) 456-3016 for prices and reservations.
Boat and bike rentals (Lac Philippe): Call (819) 456-3555.
Boat rentals (Lac La Pêche): Call (819) 456-3494.

☞ **GETTING THERE**

➤ By car, take Wellington St. east (its name changes to Rideau St.) to King Edward Ave. and go north across the Macdonald-Cartier Bridge. Follow Autoroute 5 N. to Exit 13 and go west on Old Chelsea Rd. The Visitor Centre is on the right just after Scott Rd. Free and pay parking on site. About 15 minutes from Parliament Hill. (The Visitor Centre is scheduled to move to 33 Scott Rd. in August 1999.)

➤ By bicycle, take Wellington St. west and go north across the Chaudière Bridge to Laurier St. Follow Laurier west (it becomes Alexandre-Taché Blvd.) to the Gatineau Park Pathway and go north.

☞ **COMMENT**

➤ Operated by the National Capital Commission.

or Lac La Pêche sectors further northwest. Lac Philippe has two swimming beaches and two campgrounds. Canoes, row boats and mountain bikes can be rented, and the Lusk Cave is nearby, waiting to be explored by spelunkers. There is a swimming beach at Lac La Pêche and canoe-camping is offered.

The fun doesn't stop in winter. The park has 200 kilometres of cross-country ski trails, and there are shelters along the way for winter campers. Kick-sleds, baby gliders and snowshoes can be rented at the Visitor Centre.

Camping Out at FITZROY PROVINCIAL PARK

CANON SMITH RD.
FITZROY HARBOUR
(613) 623-5159

Fitzroy Provincial Park is an ideal location for a family outing, be it an afternoon swim, a day trip or a few days of camping. A short drive from town, this small riverside park boasts the best two swimming beaches along the Ottawa River. The sand is fine and clean and the water is warm and clear. Better still, the bottom falls away gradually, so these beaches are great for the non-swimmers in your group.

The changing rooms and toilets at the swimming areas are well-maintained. Telephones, an ice-cream stand and a general store that rents canoes are nearby. The park also has a playground, picnic tables (some are shaded) and large grassy fields for games.

Fitzroy offers hikers several kilometres of trails that wind through century-old white pine forests. Pack binoculars. Goldfinches, flickers, warblers and

☞ **SEASONS AND TIMES**
➤ May 14–Oct 31.

☞ **COST**
➤ Swimming only: $7.50 per car. Campsites: May–June and Sept–Oct, $9.75, July–Aug, $14.75 to $17.75. Free parking and beach access for campers. Ontario seniors 25% discount, people with disabilities 50% discount.
Credit cards accepted.

☞ **GETTING THERE**
➤ By car, take O'Connor St. south to Hwy. 417 W. and access Hwy. 17 N. Take the Galetta Rd. exit (Route 22 E.) and follow the signs to the park. Pay parking on site for day swimmers. About 30 minutes from Parliament Hill.

☞ **NEARBY**
➳ Pinto Valley Ranch.

☞ **COMMENT**
➳ No lifeguards on duty. The water quality is tested weekly.

☞ **SIMILAR ATTRACTIONS**
➳ **Gatineau Park**, 318 Meech Lake Rd., Chelsea, Québec (819) 827-2020. (page 155.)
➳ **Rideau River Provincial Park**, Regional Rd. 13, five kilometres north of Kemptville (613) 258-2740.
➳ **Voyageur Provincial Park**, Exit 5 off Hwy. 417, Chute-a-Blondeau (near Hawkesbury) (613) 674-2825.

other songbirds reside in these woods. If you're camping, you'll have 235 campsites to choose from. Some have electrical hookup and all are wheelchair accessible. Bring insect repellent.

Nature at Its Best
THE MER BLEUE CONSERVATION AREA

RIDGE RD.
GLOUCESTER
(613) 239-5000 OR **1-800-465-1867**

Wetlands are magical places. A prime example is the Mer Bleue Conservation Area, where on cool spring and fall mornings the bog is blanketed by a bluish mist, reminding early French settlers of the blue sea. Located in the

Greenbelt southeast of town, the conservation area comprises a peat bog, marshes and a rare southern example of boreal forest, where visitors will find stunted tamarack trees and black spruce as well as carnivorous pitcher plants, Labrador tea and many other flora. If you're lucky, you might glimpse native wildlife such as beaver and deer, or a hungry chickadee might land on your hand looking for food.

Seven trails crisscross the area, offering nearly 20 kilometres of hiking and cross-country skiing. The Mer Bleue Trail, easy to walk and just over a kilometre long, is your best bet for kids. It includes a boardwalk that winds through the bog over five-metre-thick spongy peat moss. Bilingual explanatory panels are posted along the way. Bring insect repellent if you visit during bug season.

☞ **SEASONS AND TIMES**
➤ Year-round: Daily, 8 am–9 pm.

☞ **COST**
➤ Free.

☞ **GETTING THERE**
➤ By car, take Wellington St. east (its name changes to Rideau St., then Montreal Rd.) to Aviation Pkwy. and go south. After the Hwy. 417 E. merge, exit at Walkley Rd. and continue to Ridge Rd. Drive east to the parking lot. Limited free parking on site. About 20 minutes from Parliament Hill.

☞ **NEARBY**
➤ Carlsbad Forest Reserve, Carlsbad Springs Historic Site, National Museum of Science and Technology.

☞ **COMMENT**
➤ Operated by the National Capital Commission. Plan at least a 1-hour visit.

☞ **SIMILAR ATTRACTION**
➤ **Alfred Bog Walk**
(near Hawkesbury). South Nation Conservation Society (613) 948-2948. www.nation.on.ca

Fresh Air and Fun at JACQUES-CARTIER PARK

RUE LAURIER (LAURIER ST.) (BETWEEN THE ALEXANDRA AND MACDONALD-CARTIER
BRIDGES)
HULL, QUÉBEC
(819) 595-7997 OR **1-800-465-1867**
INFO@NCC-CCN.CA
VILLE.HULL.QC.CA/TOURISME

T his park is a summertime haven for cyclists and walkers. The popular Voyageurs Pathway, which follows the Ottawa River, runs through it, offering users terrific views of the Ottawa skyline and Rideau Falls. The Maison du Vélo—a great resource centre for cyclists—is also located here. Regardless of your destination, if you're travelling by bike, staff will help you plan your route.

During Winterlude (page 212), bundle up the family and head for the Snowflake Kingdom, which is located in the park. This wintry wonderland is probably the best place for children during the festivities. There are loads of fun activities and attractions for kids, including snow sculptures, outdoor games, concerts and

☞ **SEASONS AND TIMES**
→ Park: Year-round, daily, dawn to dusk.
Snowflake Kingdom: First three weeks in February, Wed—Sat, 10:30 am—8 pm; Sun, until 6 pm.

☞ **COST**
→ Free for most activities (sleigh rides extra).

☞ **GETTING THERE**
→ By car, take Wellington St. east to Sussex Dr. and go north over the Alexandra Bridge. Turn east on Laurier St. and immediately turn south into Jacques-Cartier Park. Limited free parking. During Winterlude, free parking is available at the Robert Guertin Arena (St-Redempteur St. and Allard St. in Hull) and there is a free shuttle to the site. Minutes from Parliament Hill.

films shown on screens made of snow. They can whiz down snow slides, explore a snow maze, go for a sleigh ride or, if they're 12 or under, ride on a dogsled. Bring your skates to take advantage of the outdoor rink and a sled to haul your gear on. When little teeth begin to chatter, steer your kids to the Maison Hulloise, where they can warm up while making mobiles.

Delightfully Inviting
BAXTER CONSERVATION AREA

CARTER RD. (OFF DILWORTH RD.)
KARS
(613) 489-3592 OR 1-800-267-3504
WENDT@ICONS.NET
WWW3.SYMPATICO.CA/RIDEAUCA/BAXTER2.HTML

Kids will love their visit to this conservation area, even if it's just to swim at the beach. But there's much more to do here, beginning with a self-guided nature walk. The centre has five kilometres of trails that wind through mixed conifer forest, alder thickets and

☞ **SEASONS AND TIMES**
➤ Park: Year-round, 8:30 am—8:30 pm (until sunset in winter). McManus Centre: Call for opening hours.

☞ **COST**
➤ Admission: $5 per vehicle, $2 per person on foot, annual pass $35. School programs: $3.25 per student per half-day program. Nature Day Camp: $105 a week per child.

☞ **GETTING THERE**
➤ By car, take O'Connor St. south and follow the signs for Hwy. 417 W. Take Exit 132 and access Hwy. 416 S. toward Kemptville. Take Exit 42 and go east on Dilworth Rd. After about three kilometres you'll see a sign to the centre on your right. Pay parking on site (included in the admission fee). About 40 minutes from Parliament Hill.

☞ **NEARBY**
➤ Reptile Rainforest, Watson's Mill.

☞ **COMMENT**
➤ Operated by the Rideau Valley Conservation Authority. All-terrain wheelchairs are available (call ahead). Plan a 3-hour visit.

marshland. There's also a nut grove to explore, where ginkgo, Chinese chestnut and other southerly species are found. Be sure to take in the wildflower gardens and the working displays of solar and wind power. In the winter, the park is open for snowshoeing and cross-country skiing, and there is a small hill for tobogganing.

Students of all ages can take outdoor education courses at the McManus Education Centre, which is located on site. While the topics vary from season to season, each session promises fun while learning about nature. In summer, kids ages 6 to 12 can attend Nature Day Camp. They'll do nature crafts, play organized games and go swimming and hiking.

Playing King of the Castle at
STRATHCONA PARK

LAURIER AVE. AND CHARLOTTE ST.
OTTAWA
(613) 244-5300 EXT. 3183

Stretching south from Laurier Avenue, Strathcona Park graces the western shores of the Rideau River. While parents are content to enjoy the vistas and relax under old shade trees, children by far prefer the play area, which has a wading pool, playground and the ruins of a castle. Constructed of concrete, the ruins are fun to explore. Inside, your children will find a long slide and a scattering of half-hidden statuettes of rabbits and pigs and other animals.

The park has a magnificent water fountain, paved walking paths and grassy playing fields. In one area, picnic tables edge the water, and you may be lucky enough to see ducks or swans as you eat your lunch. Just across from the park, on Range Road, are a number of foreign embassies. In summer, Odyssey Theatre performs its plays under the stars in Strathcona Park (page 125).

☞ **SEASONS AND TIMES**
➤ Year-round: Daily, 7am–10 pm.

☞ **COST**
➤ Free.

☞ **GETTING THERE**
➤ By car, take Elgin St. south to Laurier Ave., turn east and continue to Range Rd. Free parking on site. Minutes from downtown.
➤ By public transit, take OC Transpo bus 5.
➤ By bicycle or foot, follow the car directions. It's about a 30-minute walk from Parliament Hill.

☞ **NEARBY**
➤ Laurier House.

☞ **COMMENT**
➤ Operated by the City of Ottawa.

Go Wild in the City at
NEW EDINBURGH PARK

CORNER OF STANLEY AVE. AND DUFFERIN RD.
OTTAWA
(613) 244-5300 EXT. 3183

N ew Edinburgh Park is a peaceful sanctuary where visitors can escape the hustle and bustle of downtown. Hugging the eastern bank of the Rideau River south of Sussex Drive, much of the park is in its natural state. On a good day, you'll see blue herons, muskrats, turtles and groundhogs in the woods and along the river bank. Keep your eyes peeled for butterflies as well, as the park includes a butterfly garden. Walking trails follow the waterfront and picnic tables are scattered throughout. There is a playground with swings, slides and other equipment. In winter, you can go skating on the outdoor rink. Remember to bring binoculars, drinking water and insect repellent.

☞ SEASONS AND TIMES
→ Year-round: Daily, 7 am—10 pm.

☞ COST
→ Free.

☞ GETTING THERE
→ By car, go east on Wellington St. to Sussex Dr. and turn north. After crossing the Rideau River, turn south on Stanley Ave. and continue to Dufferin Rd. Free parking on site. About 10 minutes from Parliament Hill.
→ By public transit, take OC Transpo bus 3 to Dufferin Rd.
→ By bicycle, use the car directions. The park is on the Rideau River Pathway.

☞ NEARBY
→ 24 Sussex Drive (the Prime Minister's residence), Rideau Hall, Rockcliffe Park, Rideau Falls Park, Canadian War Museum, National Gallery of Canada, Royal Canadian Mint.

☞ COMMENT
→ Operated by the City of Ottawa.

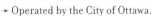

Stopping to Smell the Flowers at
ROCKCLIFFE PARK

CORNER OF ROCKCLIFFE PKWY. AND PRINCESS AVE.
OTTAWA
(613) 239-5000 OR 1-800-465-1867

A stone's throw from the residence of the Prime Minister, this urban wooded refuge is nestled between the well-to-do village of Rockcliffe Park—home to many ambassadors—and the banks of the Ottawa River. Stroll, pedal or in-line skate along the Ottawa River Pathway, where several openings in the trees afford spectacular vistas of the river and the Gatineau Hills beyond. Or drive to the lookout for a magnificent view. In season, you're likely to spot sailboats or sport fishers. Farther east, off the Rockcliffe Parkway, are the Rockeries, which in warmer months are bursting with tulips, daffodils and other flowers. Bring a camera when you come. For picnickers, the park has a well-maintained picnic site complete with stone shelter.

☞ **SEASONS AND TIMES**
➤ Year-round: Dawn to dusk.

☞ **COST**
➤ Free.

☞ **GETTING THERE**
➤ By car, take Wellington St. east to Sussex Dr. and go north. It becomes Rockcliffe Pkwy. Free parking on site. Minutes from Parliament Hill.
➤ By public transit, take OC Transpo bus 4.

☞ **NEARBY**
➤ Rideau Hall, 24 Sussex Drive (the Prime Minister's residence), RCMP Stables, Rideau Falls Park, New Edinburgh Park.

☞ **COMMENT**
➤ Operated by the National Capital Commission.

Taking a Breather at
ST. LUKE PARK

CORNER OF ELGIN ST. AND GLADSTONE AVE.
OTTAWA
(613) 244-5300 EXT. 3183

A friendly neighbourhood oasis, St. Luke Park is situated amid the many shops and restaurants that line trendy Elgin Street. If you're touring the area with young children, perhaps returning from the Canadian Museum of Nature, it's minutes away by foot and the perfect place to take a break.

Clean and well-maintained, St. Luke is a beautiful setting for an impromptu picnic. Many of the park's picnic tables are shaded by mature silver maple trees. You can order take-out from a nearby restaurant or sample the goods at one of the area's many ethnic groceries. After eating, your children can play in the playground or paddling pool. Or they might enjoy watching a pickup basketball game that is part of the everyday scene at the park.

☞ **SEASONS AND TIMES**
➤ Year-round: Daily, 7 am–10 pm.

☞ **COST**
➤ Free.

☞ **GETTING THERE**
➤ By car, take Elgin St. south to Gladstone Ave. Street parking. Minutes from Parliament Hill.
➤ By public transit, take OC Transpo bus 5.
➤ By bicycle, follow the Rideau Canal Pathway (west side) and access Gladstone Ave.
➤ By foot, follow the bicycle directions. About a 25-minute walk from Parliament Hill.

☞ **NEARBY**
➤ Canadian Museum of Nature, Rideau Canal, Minto Park.

☞ **COMMENT**
➤ Operated by the City of Ottawa.

Soaking Up the Spray at
RIDEAU FALLS PARK

OFF SUSSEX DR. (AT THE OTTAWA AND RIDEAU RIVERS)
OTTAWA
(613) 239-5000 OR **1-800-465-1867**
INFO@NCC-CCN.CA
WWW.CAPCAN.CA

E ven without the falls, this charming little park is a pleasant destination for your family. It has walking paths, well-tended flower gardens and immaculately landscaped surroundings that offer picnickers picturesque views of the Ottawa and Rideau rivers. The Rideau Falls simply enhance the park's appeal. For the best view, access the foot bridge that spans the Rideau River just before it plunges some 30 metres into the Ottawa River below. Kids will love feeling the cool spray on their faces. There are safety rails on the bridge, but be mindful that curious youngsters don't stray too far. The falls are lit up in the evening, creating a magical sight.

The Canada and the World Interpretation Centre is also found here, though it's closed in 1999. It has interactive and nar-

☞ **SEASONS AND TIMES**
➤ Park: Year-round, dawn to dusk.
Canada and the World Interpretation Centre: Call for re-opening date.

☞ **COST**
➤ Free.

☞ **GETTING THERE**
➤ By car, go east on Wellington St. to Sussex Dr. and turn north. Immediately after crossing the Rideau River look for the park on your left. Limited free parking beside the French Embassy (weekdays) and behind the National Research Council (weekends). About five minutes from Parliament Hill.
➤ By public transit, take OC Transpo bus 3 or the 13 bus during rush hour.
➤ By bicycle or foot, use the car directions. It's about a 30-minute walk from Parliament Hill.

☞ **NEARBY**
➤ 24 Sussex Drive (the Prime Minister's residence), Rideau Hall, Rockcliffe Park, New Edinburgh Park, Canadian War Museum, National Gallery of Canada, Royal Canadian Mint.

☞ **COMMENT**
➤ Operated by the National Capital Commission.

rative exhibits that look at Canada's global achievements. It also presents a Sunday Picnic series that organizes concerts and activities for families.

Other Green Spaces

Andrew Haydon Park

ACRES RD. AND CARLING AVE. • NEPEAN
(613) 727-6641 • WWW.CITY.NEPEAN.ON.CA/PARKS/PARKS1.HTM

L iven up those lazy summer days with a visit to Andrew Haydon Park on the Ottawa River, where children love to frolic in the water under sprinklers and jets, dig in the sand or explore such thematic play areas as a ship with rope ladders and swings. The park has picnic sites with barbecues, walking paths, ponds, streams and a waterfall, and there is an outdoor bandstand where shows are performed (check the Web site for upcoming attractions). The Nepean Sailing Club is based here. In winter, the park is a popular destination for cross-country skiers.

☞ Year-round: Daily, dawn to dusk.
☞ Free.

☞ Take the Ottawa River Pkwy. west to Richmond Rd. and go west to Carling Ave. Take Carling west to Acres Rd. About 25 minutes from Parliament Hill.

☞ Take OC Transpo bus 166.

Lac-Beauchamp Park

745, BOUL. MALONEY (MALONEY BLVD.) • GATINEAU, QUÉBEC • (819) 669-2548

Lac Beauchamp Park, located in the heart of the city of Gatineau, offers families a range of year-round activities. The swimming beach is popular in the summertime, and canoes and pedal boats can be rented. Hikers and bicyclists can travel on 12 kilometres of paths that wind through the wooded parkland, which is home to a variety of bird life. In winter, bring your skates for the lake, cross-country skis for the trails and toboggans for the hill. A snack bar and toilets are located in the pavilion.

☞ Year-round: Mon—Fri, 8 am—9 pm; weekends, 9 am—9 pm.

☞ Fees for some activities.

☞ Take the Macdonald-Cartier Bridge and access Rte. 148 E. (Maloney Blvd. in Gatineau) and continue to the park. About 20 minutes from Parliament Hill.

Leamy Lake Park

80, BOUL. FOURNIER (FOURNIER BLVD.) • HULL, QUÉBEC
(613) 239-5000 OR 1-800-465-1867 • WWW.CAPCAN.CA

Like other parks on the Ottawa River, this one has an attractive swimming beach, well-maintained picnic areas and several kilometres of trails that meander through woods and fields. Bring your bicycles to take advantage of the pathways that run through the park. You can see the Prime Minister's residence across the river and there is a good view of Rideau Falls. An archaeological dig is located here and can be visited, though it's closed for 1999. Call the National Capital Commission for the re-opening date.

☞ Year-round: Daily, dawn to dusk.
☞ Free.
☞ Take the Macdonald-Cartier Bridge and access Rte. 148 E. Continue east across the Leamy Creek Bridge and take the first exit south. Some free parking near the beach. About 10 minutes from Parliament Hill.

Brantwood Park

ONSLOW CR. (BETWEEN ELLIOT AVE. AND CLEGG ST.) • OTTAWA
(613) 244-5300 EXT. 3183

The outdoor rinks are unusual here. They're connected in a series by icy paths that are designed to be skated on. In summer, the park has a wading pool and jungle gym.

☞ Year-round: Daily, 7 am—10 pm.
☞ Free.
☞ Take Bank St. south to Sunnyside Ave. and turn east to Riverdale Ave. Go north to Main St. (Riverdale merges with Main) and continue until Clegg Ave. Turn east. Street parking. About 10 minutes from Parliament Hill.
Take OC Transpo buses 5 or 16.

Brewer Park

HOPEWELL AVE. NEAR BRONSON AVE. • OTTAWA • (613) 244-5300 EXT. 3183

In summer, children make a beeline for the water park, which has water sprays, jets and slides. There is also a playground designed especially for tots. The park has an arena and pool, baseball dia-monds, picnic areas and walking paths near the

Rideau River. In winter, grab your skates and do a few laps on the speed-skating oval. It's open to the public. Lessons are available.

☞   Year-round: Daily, 7 am—10 pm.
☞   Free.
☞   Take Bronson Ave. south to Hopewell Ave. and turn east into the park. Free parking. About 10 minutes from Parliament Hill. Take OC Transpo buses 4, 7 or 118.

Vincent Massey Park

HERON RD. (WEST OF RIVERSIDE DR.) • OTTAWA • (613) 244-5300 EXT. 3183

T his large park has playing fields, recreational paths, wooded sections, picnic sites with barbecues and drinking fountains. There are also well-maintained toilets. Lying immediately south is Hog's Back Falls Park (Hog's Back Road at Colonel By Drive), which offers visitors picnic areas, walking trails, woods and excellent views of Hog's Back Falls on the Rideau River (also known as Prince of Wales Falls). Toilets and a snack bar are nearby. If your family is interested in a swim at the beach, continue south on Riverside Drive to Ridgewood Avenue, where you'll find Mooney's Bay Park. It has a sandy swimming beach, a playground, shade trees, picnic tables, a snack bar and toilets. There is pay parking in the summer.

☞   Year-round: Daily, 7 am—10 pm.
☞   Free.
☞   Take Bronson Ave. south to Heron Rd. and go west to Vincent Massey Park. Pay parking in the summer. About 15 minutes from Parliament Hill.
☞   Take OC Transpo buses 87, 111, 118 or 146.

Major's Hill Park

MACKENZIE AVE. (BEHIND THE CHÂTEAU LAURIER) • OTTAWA
(613) 239-5000 OR 1-800-465-1867 • WWW.CAPCAN.CA

Created in the early 1870s, this is Ottawa's oldest park. From here you can see the Parliament Buildings, the Rideau Canal and the Ottawa River. In summer, the park hosts craft fairs and concerts and is a major venue for events that celebrate the Canadian Tulip Festival and Canada Day. The Astrolabe Theatre is located at the tip of the park, behind the National Gallery of Canada. Music festivals and other shows are held at the charming outdoor amphitheatre in the spring and summer.

☞ Year-round: Daily, dawn to dusk.
☞ Free.
☞ Take Wellington St. east to Mackenzie Ave. and go north. Minutes from Parliament Hill.
☞ Take OC Transpo buses 3 or 306.

The Greenbelt

NATIONAL CAPITAL COMMISSION • 40 ELGIN ST. • OTTAWA
(613) 239-5000 OR 1-800-465-1867 • WWW.CAPCAN.CA

The Greenbelt is so big, it can't be seen in a single day. So visitors come back again and again, eager to explore the nearly 100 kilometres of hiking and cross-country skiing trails that wind through the 200 square kilometres of forests, wetlands, farmland and river shoreline that make up this region. Newcomers to the Greenbelt should buy an all-season trail map ($3) at the Capital Infocentre at 90 Wellington Street. It will tell you which trails are designated for hiking and which ones are best for skiing and snowshoeing. Some trails include sec-

tions of the Trans Canada Trail and the Rideau Trail,
which links Ottawa and Kingston. The map will also
show you where to find parking. There are picnic
areas along some of the trails, so bring a lunch.
Binoculars are a good idea as the Greenbelt is full of
wildlife.

☞   Year-round: Daily.

☞   Free.

☞   A few of the seven sectors that make up the Greenbelt are
accessible from major highways. Call the National Capital
Commission for directions or refer to the trail map.

CHAPTER 9

HISTORICAL SITES

The Ottawa Valley has changed considerably over the past 160 years and there's no better way for children to learn about the history of the area than to visit the heritage and historical sites that are listed in this chapter. Your family can witness turn-of-the-century rural life at the Cumberland Heritage Village Museum. At the Fort Wellington National Historic Site, you can experience how soldiers lived in the 1860s. To learn about the hardships faced by the men who constructed the Rideau Canal, visit the Bytown Museum. And there's much more. The Billings Estate Museum, Laurier House, the Mackenzie King Estate and Watson's Mill have their own stories to tell that will not only engage your children, but will keep them asking for more.

NOTE
These historical sites, which are found elsewhere in this guide, also welcome children:
Parliament Hill (Chapter 1, page 32)
Rideau Hall (Chapter 1, page 24)
Rideau Canal (Chapter 1, page 27)
Ottawa Locks (Chapter 1, page 34)
Pinhey's Point (Chapter 2, page 52)
Upper Canada Village (Chapter 12, page 223)

Eating Freshly Baked Cookies at the CUMBERLAND HERITAGE VILLAGE MUSEUM

2940 QUEEN ST.
CUMBERLAND
(613) 833-3059
WWW.MUNICIPALITY.CUMBERLAND.ON.CA

Instead of hearing about the good old days, children can live them at the Cumberland Heritage Village Museum, a 40-hectare site that offers a glimpse into lower Ottawa Valley life in the early 1900s. Just behind the train station, which serves as the admissions office and general store, you'll find over 25 historic buildings, many of which were moved to the museum from nearby communities. The whole family is welcome to explore most of the buildings (for wheelchair accessibility, look for ramps at the back entrances).

You can walk the gravel paths or take a

☞ **SEASONS AND TIMES**
➤ May 15—Thanksgiving Day, Tue—Fri, 11 am—5 pm; weekends, 10 am—5 pm.

☞ **COST**
➤ Adults $5, seniors and students $3, children under 4 free, families $12. Credit cards accepted.

☞ **GETTING THERE**
➤ By car, take Rideau St. to County Rd. 174 (formerly Hwy. 17 E.) and drive to Cumberland. At Cameron St. turn south to Queen St., then go east. Watch for the museum on your right. Free parking on site. About 25 minutes from Parliament Hill.
➤ By bicycle, take Sussex Dr. north to Rockcliffe Pkwy. and cross Hwy. 17. Turn north onto St. Joseph St. (its name will change to Queen St.). About a 30-kilometre ride from Parliament Hill.

☞ **COMMENT**

➤ To avoid drinking water that tastes of sulphur, use the water cooler. Bilingual staff. Diaper-changing facilities. Plan a 3-hour visit.

wagon ride to visit a one-room schoolhouse, a black-smith's forge, a sawmill, a gas station, a church and several homes. Kids will be delighted playing in the old-fashioned playground and visiting the petting zoo. Actors dressed in period costume will be your guides. Feel free to ask them questions. The farmer's wife may even offer you some freshly baked cookies and biscuits.

Bring a lunch and enjoy the spacious and grassy picnic area, which has tables that are sheltered. The museum also has facilities for receptions and children's birthday parties.

Playing Soldiers at FORT WELLINGTON NATIONAL HISTORIC SITE

COUNTY RD. 2
PRESCOTT
(613) 925-2896
KIM_ROBINSON@PCH.GC.CA

To find out what it was like to be a soldier in the last century, visit Fort Wellington. This child-friendly museum is geared for families. Interpreters dressed in period costume will lead groups from the Visitors Centre on a one-hour tour of the block-house, officers' quarters, latrine and caponnière, where you'll see displays of clothing, weapons and fur-niture. Since many of the items are reproductions, it's okay to handle them.

Constructed by the British during the War of 1812 to guard vital shipping routes from American attacks, the fort is equipped with palisades, a dry moat and cannon. On the third floor of the blockhouse is a scale model of the garrison and panels detailing its history. There are also uni-forms for the kids to try on. Fort Wellington has educa-tional programs for stu-dents of all ages that include tours, activities and in-class study sessions using artifacts from the fort. Day camps are held in July and August.

☞ **SEASONS AND TIMES**

→ May 23—Sept 30, daily, 10 am—5 pm. Other times by appointment only.

☞ **COST**

→ Adults $3, seniors $2.50, youth (6 to 16) $1.50, children under 5 free.

☞ **GETTING THERE**

→ By car, take O'Connor St. south to Laurier Ave. and go west. Turn south on Bronson Ave. to access Hwy. 16 S. Continue to County Rd. 2 (formerly Hwy. 2) and go west. The fort is on the right just off the highway. Free parking on site. About one hour from Parliament Hill.

☞ **COMMENT**

→ Operated by Canadian Heritage, Parks Canada. Wheelchair and stroller access to the Visitors Centre and the main floor of the block-house. Plan a 3-hour visit.

☞ **SIMILAR ATTRACTION**

→ **Fort Henry**, **Kingston**. Interactive displays, artifacts, military drills and parades in a 19th-century fort. County Rd. 2 (formerly Hwy. 2) at Hwy. 15, Kingston (613) 542-7388 or 1-800-437-2233. www.parks.on.ca

Celebrating Summer at MACKENZIE KING ESTATE

72, RUE BARNES (BARNES ST.)
CHELSEA, QUÉBEC
(819) 827-2020 OR 1-800-465-1867
GPVISITO@NCC-CCN.CA
WWW.CAPCAN.CA

W illiam Lyon Mackenzie King, Canada's tenth prime minister, used this lovely estate in Gatineau Park as a retreat during the first half of this century. Visitors can tour Moorside cottage, where King lived. It has a tearoom and restaurant on the main floor, and upstairs you'll find displays of King's personal belongings. As you stroll through the grounds, which have been restored to their condition during King's residency, you'll come across Kingswood cottage, a boathouse, gardens and a beautiful collection of ruins which King had assembled.

If your children are small, it might be best to visit during one of the regularly scheduled summer events, when they can

☞ **SEASONS AND TIMES**
➤ Victoria Day—Thanksgiving, daily, 10 am—6 pm.

☞ **COST**
➤ Pedestrians and bicyclists: Free. Cars: $6.
Scheduled events: Charges vary.

☞ **GETTING THERE**
➤ By car, take Wellington St. east (it becomes Rideau St.) and go north on King Edward Ave. Cross the Macdonald-Cartier Bridge to Autoroute 5 N. and continue to the town of Chelsea. Turn west onto Old Chelsea Rd. (it becomes Meech Lake Rd.) and follow it to the Gatineau Pkwy. Turn south and follow the posted signs to the estate. Pay parking on site. About 25 minutes from Parliament Hill.

☞ **COMMENT**
➤ Operated by the National Capital Commission. Plan a 3-hour visit.

have their faces painted, make crafts and listen to live music. Featured are the Flower Celebration, the Ghost Walk, the Garden Party and other events. While picnics are not permitted on the grounds, there are picnic areas in the park surrounding the estate. Meech Lake is just a few kilometres to the north, so bring your swimsuits if it's a hot day.

Discovering Antique Toys at the BYTOWN MUSEUM

BESIDE THE OTTAWA LOCKS OF THE RIDEAU CANAL
OTTAWA
(613) 234-4570

O ttawa's oldest stone building is the ideal location for a museum that presents the history of Bytown. Erected in 1827, the Commissariat housed a treasury for the payroll of the builders of the Rideau Canal and a storehouse for their equipment.

Your tour will begin at the canal-builders exhibit, where photographs, mannequins and posters depict the hardships the labourers encountered as they sweated over the project.

> ☞ **SEASONS AND TIMES**
> → Spring: April 5—May 9, Mon—Fri, 10 am—4 pm.
> Summer: May 10—Oct 11, Mon—Sat, 10 am—5 pm; Sun, 1 pm—5 pm.
> Fall: Oct 14—Nov 26, Mon—Fri, 10 am—4 pm.
> Winter: Nov 29—Mar 31, Mon—Fri, 8 am—4 pm (by appointment).
>
> ☞ **COST**
> → Adults $2.50, students $1.25, children 11 and under $0.50, families $6.

☞ **GETTING THERE**

➤ By car, take Wellington St. east and park near the Château Laurier. It's a short walk north along the canal.

➤ By public transit, take OC Transpo buses 1 through 7.

➤ By bicycle, take the Rideau Canal Pathway north, or pedal from the north end of Major's Hill Park.

➤ By foot, follow Wellington St. east and descend the steps from the bridge to the canal. The museum is a few minutes walk north.

☞ **NEARBY**

➤ The Ottawa Locks, Parliament Hill, Major's Hill Park, Canadian Museum of Contemporary Photography, National War Memorial.

☞ **COMMENT**

➤ Operated by the Historical Society of Ottawa. Mainly narrative exhibits. Plan a 1-hour visit.

Although this exhibition is free, visitors must pay to access other parts of the museum. Upstairs there is a display featuring Lieutenant-Colonel John By, the canal's chief engineer. You can watch a short video about him and view his personal effects, which include furniture, engineering instruments and some of his sketches. The museum also houses faithful recreations of a pioneer kitchen, a Victorian parlour and a lumbermen's shanty. More interesting to children will be the porcelain dolls, toy soldiers and other playthings that are on view in the antique toy store.

A Family's Life in the 1800s
at the
BILLINGS ESTATE MUSEUM

2100 CABOT ST.
OTTAWA
(613) 247-4830
BEMCHIN@OTT.HOOKUP.NET

Very old and very elegant, Billings house welcomes visitors with an interest in family histories and days gone by. Constructed in 1827-1828 by Braddish and Lamira Billings, two of Bytown's earliest residents, the well-preserved frame house features a range of narrative exhibits, complete with family furnishings, tools, paintings and photographs, that recount the Billings' story through five generations. Guided tours are offered or you can explore on your own. Leave time to investigate the four hectares of lush grounds that surround the house, where you'll find flower gardens, woods, the family cemetery and a picnic area. On Wednesday, Thursday and Sunday

☞ **SEASONS AND TIMES**
➤ May 1—Oct 31, Tue—Sun, 12 pm—5 pm.
Year-round visits for groups with reservations.

☞ **COST**
➤ Adults $2.50, seniors $2, youth (5 to 17) $1.50, under 5 free.

☞ **GETTING THERE**
➤ By car, take Bank St. south to Riverside Dr. and go east to Pleasant Park Rd. Turn south to Cabot St. and follow the posted museum signs. Free parking on site. About 15 minutes from Parliament Hill.
➤ By public transit, take OC Transpo buses 87, 96, 97 or 149.
➤ By bicycle, follow the Rideau River Eastern Pathway.

☞ **NEARBY**
➤ Vincent Massey Park, Hog's Back Falls Park and Mooney's Bay Park.

☞ **COMMENT**
➤ The second floor is inaccessible to wheelchairs. Diaper-changing facilities. Operated by the City of Ottawa. Plan a 1-hour visit.

☞ **SIMILAR ATTRACTION**
➤ **Heritage House Museum,** Smiths Falls. Tours, special events, workshops and children's programs in a Victorian-era home. 11 Old Slys Road, Smiths Falls (613) 283-8560.

afternoons in the summer, tea and scones are served on the lawn.

Of particular interest to children are Family Day, the Blacksmiths' Fair and periodic events that feature art workshops and storytelling. The museum also has educational programs for kids from 5 to 11 (tours, model building, observation games) and Heritage To Go kits (antique clothing and toys) to loan to schools ($4 a week). For information about programs and events, call 247-4830.

Going Back in Time at LAURIER HOUSE NATIONAL HISTORIC SITE

335 Laurier Ave. E.
Ottawa
(613) 992-8142

M ost kids won't care that Canada's wartime prime minister, William Lyon Mackenzie King, used a crystal ball to determine state affairs. They'll just want to see one. King's famous glass orb is among several of his possessions on display at stately Laurier House. The museum also has memorabilia and furnishings of prime ministers Wilfrid Laurier and Lester B. Pearson.

Several rooms of the three-storey house have been restored to their condition during the first half of this century, when it was first Laurier's, and then King's, official residence. You'll see Laurier's 1912 player piano (still operational) and King's extensive art collection, which includes a 4,000-year-old Sumerian clay tablet. The house also has a re-creation of Pearson's study,

☞ **SEASONS AND TIMES**
➤ Summer: Apr 1–Sept 30, Tue–Sat, 9 am–5 pm; Sun, 2 pm–5 pm. Winter: Oct 1–Mar 31, Tue–Sat, 10 am–5 pm; Sun, 2 pm–5 pm.

☞ **COST**
➤ Adults $2.25, seniors $1.75, students (6 to 16) $1.25, children under 6 free.

☞ **GETTING THERE**
➤ By car, take Elgin St. south to Laurier Ave. and turn east. Drive to Chapel St. The house is on the left. Limited free street parking (plentiful on weekends). Minutes from Parliament Hill.
➤ By public transit, take OC Transpo buses 5 or 316.
➤ By bicycle or foot, follow the car directions. It's about a 20-minute walk.

☞ **NEARBY**
➤ Strathcona Park.

☞ **COMMENT**
➤ Operated by Canadian Heritage, Parks Canada. Plan a 2-hour visit.

although he was never actually a resident. Other interesting items include a guest book signed by Franklin Roosevelt, Charles de Gaulle and Shirley Temple, among others, chairs owned by Napoleon Bonaparte, and the plaster cast of Abraham Lincoln's face that was used to make the Lincoln Memorial in Washington.

While the attendants are willing to explain the collection's historical significance to children in an easy-to-understand manner, younger kids will prefer the playground across Chapel Street.

Ghost Busting at
WATSON'S MILL

5525 DICKINSON ST.
MANOTICK
(613) 692-2500 (SUMMER)
OR (613) 692-3571 (WINTER)
OR 1-800-267-3504
WWW3.SYMPATICO.CA/RIDEAUCA/DICKIN1.HTML

☞ **SEASONS AND TIMES**
➤ June—Aug, daily, 10 am—5 pm.
May and Sept—Oct, weekends,
10 am—5 pm.
Other times by reservation.

☞ **COST**
➤ Free (suggested donation $1).

☞ **GETTING THERE**
➤ By car, take O'Connor St. south
and turn west onto Laurier Ave. Turn
south on Bronson Ave. and access
Hwy. 16 S. (Prescott Hwy.). Turn east
on Rte. 13 (Rideau Valley Dr.) and
continue to Manotick. Just after the
Bridge St. intersection, turn east
onto Mill St. and drive to the river.
Free parking on site. About 30 minutes from Parliament Hill.

☞ **COMMENT**
➤ Owned by the Rideau Valley
Conservation Authority, operated by
volunteers. Plan a 1-hour visit.

☞ **SIMILAR ATTRACTION**
➤ **Maclaren's Mill**, about 30 minutes north of Ottawa, dates from the
same period. Mill St., Wakefield,
Québec (819) 459-8868.

For kids, the mill's ghost is the main attraction. The story goes like this: Soon after the mill was built in 1860 to produce flour, the wife of one of its owners tumbled into the grinding machinery and died. Legend has it that her spirit still haunts the site. Or that's what your guide will tell you as you tour the building, which is completely restored and functional. You'll also hear about the mill's history and architecture, and you'll see the machinery in operation. After the visit, take your children to feed the ducks near the dam on the Rideau River. You can reach a small park on Manotick Island by crossing the dam.

There's a farmer's market outside the mill on Saturday mornings between May and October. Or you might want to take a few minutes to stroll through the village of Manotick, which has many heritage buildings dating from the turn of the century and earlier. There are also restaurants and boutiques.

Other Historical Sites

St. Patrick's Basilica

281 NEPEAN ST. • OTTAWA • (613) 233-1125 • WWW.BASILICA.ORG

B uilt between 1866 and 1875, St. Patrick's Basilica is Ottawa's oldest Catholic church serving the English-speaking community. Designed by Fuller and Laver, who also conceived the plans for Parliament Hill's East and West blocks, the church is constructed from local stone and its cornerstone was laid by Sir John A. Macdonald in 1872. Its Gothic interior is highlighted by the elaborately carved wooden altar of sacrifice, oak pews, marble altars and statues, a Casavant pipe organ and stencilled ceilings. While you take in the splendour, your kids can keep busy identifying the biblical stories depicted in the stained-glass windows or seeing who can count the most four-leafed clovers hidden in the decor.

☞ Year-round: Mon—Fri, 6 am—5:30 pm; Sat, 6 am—8 pm; Sun, 6 am—10 pm.

☞ Free (donations are accepted).

☞ Take Wellington St. west to Bank St. and go south to Gloucester St. Turn west. St. Patrick's is one block further down, on the corner of Gloucester and Kent. There is a small parking lot and street parking. Minutes from Parliament Hill.

☞ Take OC Transpo buses 8, 85, 86, 95, 96 or 97.

SIMILAR ATTRACTION

➤ **The Cathedral Basilica of Notre Dame**, which was built in 1839, is Ottawa's oldest surviving church. You'll find over 200 statues around the main altar, a gilded statue of the Madonna and child, a neo-Gothic interior and stained-glass windows. 385 Sussex Dr., Ottawa (613) 241-7496.

Ottawa International Hostel

75 NICHOLAS ST. • OTTAWA
(613) 235-2595 OR 1-800-461-8585 (RESERVATIONS)
HTTP://INFOWEB.MAGI.COM/~HICOE/OTTAWA.HTM

This hostel has lots of history. A heritage building that held the Carleton County Jail between 1862 and 1972, this was where the last public hanging in Canada took place in the 1960s. Guided tours include a look at the gallows, a history of the jail and descriptions of prison conditions in days gone by. You can view prisoners' cells, death row and the public stocks. The tours, which last about an hour, aren't a good idea for kids under six because of the gruesome content.

The hostel has private rooms and dormitories. Special rates are available for groups and families. Advance reservations required. The Hostel Shop on the ground floor operates a budget travel agency. Call 569-1400 for details.

☞ Year-round: Fri, 7 pm; Sat, 4 pm. Group tours can be arranged.
☞ $3 per person.
☞ Take Wellington St. east (it becomes Rideau St.) to Nicholas St. and go south. Street parking. Minutes from Parliament Hill. It's about a 10-minute walk.
☞ Take OC Transpo bus 4 to Nicholas St. and Rideau St. The hostel is two blocks south on Nicholas (toward the bridge).

Beechwood Cemetery

280 BEECHWOOD AVE. • OTTAWA • (613) 741-9530

This is one of Canada's most historic cemeteries. Buried here are Sir Robert Borden, who was Canada's prime minister from 1911 to 1920, Sir Sanford Fleming, who invented Standard Time, pulp and paper and railway baron John Boothe, and other important figures. There is an annual guided tour of the grounds. In the past it has included such themes as sports heroes, arts and literature and the roaring twenties. There is also a horticultural tour as well as self-guided tours. While you're taking in the history, your children may prefer a simpler approach—running around the well-maintained, parklike setting.

☞ Grounds: Year-round, Mon—Fri, 8 am—5 pm; weekends, 8 am—4 pm.
☞ Free.
☞ Take Wellington St. east to Sussex Dr. and go north to Murray St. Turn east and cross the St. Patrick St. Bridge to Beechwood Ave.
☞ Take OC Transpo bus 7.

The Log Farm

670 CEDARVIEW RD. • NEPEAN • (613) 825-4352

T he restored Bradley farm, which dates from 1857, is a popular destination for school groups and families. Visitors are invited to join in the spirit of the times by helping with the chores as they would have been performed in the 1870s. Self-guided tours are offered. There is a schedule of special events, seasonal activities and educational programs that include hands-on demonstrations in the sugar bush. The farm has walking trails, a petting farm and a picnic area.

☞   Summer: Mid-June—Labour Day, Wed—Sun, 10 am—4 pm.

☞   Other times: Weekends, 10 am—4 pm.

☞   Free (a donation is requested).

☞   Call for directions.

Cartier Square Drill Hall

LAURIER AVE. (BESIDE THE QUEEN ELIZABETH DRIVEWAY)
OTTAWA • (613) 990-3507

E very morning in the summer, the Governor General's Foot Guard assembles at Cartier Square Drill Hall to march to Parliament Hill for the Changing of the Guard. If you want to follow the troops on their parade route, arrive at the drill hall before 9:30 am. The small regimental museum of the Cameron Highlanders of Ottawa is located in the hall. It has displays of uniforms, weapons and photographs, as well as other exhibits.

☞   Museum visits: Year-round, Thu, 7 pm—9:30 pm, or by appointment.

☞   Free.

☞   Take O'Connor St. south to Laurier Ave. and turn east.

☞   Take OC Transpo buses 5, 6 or 14.

Chapter 10

Getting There is half the fun

I n the case of some family outings, the journey *is* the destination. In other words, the act of boating, walking, cycling, skating or travelling by train is a large part of what makes the day enjoyable and memorable for you and your kids. If you like to cycle, in-line skate or go for long walks, head for the National Capital Region's recreational pathways—a network of scenic routes that offer the opportunity to take lots of interesting side trips along the way. Anyone fond of boats will want to take a cruise on the Rideau Canal or Ottawa River. Train-lovers will find their way to Hull, where a steam-powered train makes a daily run to Chelsea. This chapter also lists other interesting travel experiences, including driving over an ice bridge, going on a bus or bike tour, visiting the airport and spending the day island hopping on the Long Sault Parkway. There's also some information about Ottawa-Hull's public transportation system. So check your energy levels, then rev up for a day of non-stop fun.

NOTE

You'll find these other fun ways to travel elsewhere in this guide:
Taking an airplane ride at the National Aviation Museum (Chapter 1, page 29).
Going for a balloon ride at the Gatineau Hot Air Balloon Festival (Chapter 11, page 210).
Riding the Via train to Smiths Falls (Chapter 12, page 228).

All Aboard the
HULL-CHELSEA-WAKEFIELD STEAM TRAIN

165 RUE DEVEAULT (DEVEAULT ST.)
HULL, QUÉBEC
(819) 778-7246 OR 1-800-871-7246

For railroad buffs, there's nothing like riding a steam train powered by an authentic 1907 locomotive. Daily during the summer season, old Number 909 departs from Hull and chugs along the scenic Gatineau River. Children are given special attention on board. They'll enjoy the tour guide's animated running commentary, and when they tire of that, can have their faces painted. They'll also be enchanted by the roving band of Québec folk musicians who visit each coach, singing with gusto as they strum their guitars.

The 90-minute ride brings the train to the pretty village of Wakefield, where passengers have a two-hour stopover. Before heading off to explore the town's attractions, you may want to visit the steam engine and watch as the crew turns it around for the trip back. That done, there is a guided walking tour of the village that's included in the ticket

☞ **SEASONS AND TIMES**

➤ June, Tues, Wed and Sun, 1:30 pm.
July—Aug, Sun—Thu, 1:30 pm; Fri—Sat, 10 am.
Dinner train 6:30—10:30 pm.

☞ **COST**

➤ Adults $26, seniors $23, students $22, children (3 to 12) $12, under 3 free, families $68, dinner train $59. Credit cards accepted. Reservations recommended.

price. When it's time to eat, whether you've packed a lunch or purchased take-out from one of many nearby eateries, you'll want to take advantage of Wakefield's beautiful riverside picnic area.

☞ **GETTING THERE**

➤ By car, take Wellington St. east (its name changes to Rideau St.) to King Edward Ave. go north and cross the Macdonald-Cartier Bridge. From Québec Hwy. 5 N. take Exit 3 (de la Carrière Blvd.), go north to Deveault St. then turn west. Free parking on site. About 15 minutes from Parliament Hill.

➤ By public transit, take STO bus 60 from the Rideau Centre (in front of Eaton's) and tell the driver your destination. The train station is a short walk from the bus stop.

☞ **COMMENT**

➤ The train coaches are air-conditioned and non-smoking.

❥ ❥ ❥

Rolling Along the CAPITAL PATHWAY NETWORK

(613) 239-5000 OR **1-800-465-1867**

Recreational pathways are a delightful and practical way for cyclists, in-line skaters, joggers and walkers to get around the National Capital Region. They extend some 170 kilometres, linking Aylmer, Gloucester, Hull, Kanata, Ottawa and Vanier in a network of scenic routes that are paved, patrolled, well maintained and closed to motorized traffic. Benches and drinking fountains are located at intervals along some of the routes. Lots of people use the pathways to get to work or school, and many major attractions,

☞ **SEASONS AND TIMES**
➤ Recreational pathways: Spring until covered with snow.

☞ **COST**
➤ Free.

☞ **COMMENT**
➤ While bicycling or in-line skating, every member of your family should be wearing approved and fitted safety headgear.

such as museums and parks, are located along them. Maps of the network are available for $2 at the Capital Infocentre at 90 Wellington Street.

For alternative routes, take to the area's parkways, some of which are closed to cars on Sunday Bikedays between Victoria Day and Labour Day. Colonel By Drive and the Ottawa River and Rockcliffe parkways are car-free from 9 am to 1 pm, while the Lac Fortune, Gatineau and Champlain parkways in Gatineau Park are reserved for cycling, in-line skating and strolling between 6 am and noon. With the exception of the challenging routes in Gatineau Park, most of the roads are fairly level, though there are a few rolling hills.

Cruising Along on
PAUL'S BOAT LINES

THE OTTAWA LOCKS AND THE HULL MARINA
OTTAWA
(613) 225-6781 OR (613) 235-8409

T aking a cruise with Paul's Boat Lines is a fun way to learn about points of interest along the Ottawa River and the Rideau Canal. The 90-minute river tours depart throughout the day from the Ottawa Locks and the Hull Marina. You'll sail past the Parliament Buildings, the Supreme Court of Canada, the Royal Canadian Mint and other landmarks. If you prefer to cruise the canal, you can choose between a 75-minute scenic round trip from the Rideau Canal Dock to Dow's Lake, or a day-long voyage to Kars (Thursdays and Fridays only).

Regardless of the route, your bilingual tour guide will provide colourful running commentary that includes interesting tidbits of information, such as how the Rideau Falls got its name (from the river it looks like a curtain, or

☞ SEASONS AND TIMES
➤ Summer: Victoria Day—Thanksgiving Day.
Departures: 10 am—8:30 pm.

☞ COST
➤ Rideau Canal: Adults $12, students and seniors $10, children $6, family of four $30.
Ottawa River: Adults $14, students and seniors $12, children $7, family of four $30. Group rates available.

☞ GETTING THERE
➤ By car, (to access the Hull Marina) take Wellington St. east to Mackenzie Ave. and go north over the Alexandra Bridge. At Laurier St. turn east. The marina is in Jacques-Cartier Park on the right. Pay parking on site. Minutes from Parliament Hill.
➤ By public transit, take OC Transpo buses 1 through 7 to the locks.
➤ By bicycle, take the Rideau Canal or Major's Hill Park paths to the locks.
➤ By foot, follow Wellington St. east and descend the stairs from the bridge to the canal. Walk north for a few minutes.

rideau in French). In case your children tire of the scenery, bring drawing paper and crayons so they can colour at the tables below deck.

> ☞ **COMMENT**
> ➤ Wheelchair and stroller access from the Hull Marina. Heated decks.
>
> ☞ **SIMILAR ATTRACTIONS**
> ➤ **The Ottawa Riverboat Company** (613) 562-4888.
> ➤ **M/S Jacques-Cartier** (819) 375-3000 or 1-800-567-3737. This all-day cruise includes a dinner and dance and isn't recommended for younger children.

Be Your Own Tour Guide
BIKE TOURS

RENTABIKE
1 RIDEAU ST.
OTTAWA
(613) 241-4140
HTTP://WWW.CYBERUS.CA~RENTABIKE/

Touring Ottawa by bicycle is a great way to see one of Canada's most beautiful cities. But don't be discouraged if you don't have your own wheels. RentABike has a bicycle for every member of the family, as well as tandem bicycles, bicycle trailers and trail-a-bikes. They'll also help you plan a route. The company has eight scenic tours to choose from, including routes that wind through Gatineau Park or follow the Rideau Canal or Ottawa River. The tours range from two hours long to a half-day. RentABike provides helmets, locks and maps at no extra charge. Bike racks are available for rental. Group tours can be arranged.

☞ **SEASONS AND TIMES**
➤ Apr 1—May 15, daily, 9 am—6 pm.
May 16—Sept 15, daily, 9 am—8 pm.
Sept 16—Oct 30, daily, 9 am—6 pm.

☞ **COST**
➤ Bike rentals start at $7 an hour. Credit card required. Family and group discounts available.

☞ **GETTING THERE**
➤ By car or foot, take Wellington St. east to the Château Laurier. RentABike is located behind the hotel.

☞ **NEARBY**
➤ Parliament Hill, Ottawa Locks, Bytown Museum, ByWard Market, Major's Hill Park.

☞ **SIMILAR ATTRACTIONS**
➤ **Maison de Vélo** (in Jacques-Cartier Park). This cyclist's resource centre lends out bikes at no charge (identification is required). Maps and advice on planning routes are available. 350, rue Laurier, Hull, Québec (819) 997-4356. http://www.ville.hull.qc.ca/tourisme/mvelo/htm
➤ **Cyco's Inc.**
5 Hawthorne Ave., Ottawa • (613) 567-8180.
➤ **National Capital Cycling**
75 Nicholas St., Ottawa (Ottawa International Hostel) • (613) 234-9770.
➤ **RentABike Vélocation**
Holiday Inn Plaza La Chaudière, Hull, Québec
(819) 778-3880 • http://www.cyberus.ca/~rentabike/

☞ **COMMENT**
➤ If you're looking to buy, the bike rental agencies sell off all their equipment each fall. Put your name down early as inventory disappears quickly.

The Wheels on the Bus Go Round and Round
BUS TOURS

N othing beats a bus tour if you want an overview of Ottawa-Hull. You'll get an introduction to Parliament Hill, the Museum of Civilization, Rideau Hall, the National Gallery of Canada, ByWard Market, Dow's Lake and other points of interest. Two companies, Gray Line and Capital Double Decker & Trolley Tours, offer passenger excursions that last about two hours. A bilingual guide provides running commentary and there are brief stops along the way. Both companies have "hop on, hop off" tickets for passengers who want to leave the tour at designated stops and spend time exploring the sights. The tickets entitle their bearers to resume the tour on a later bus and can be used over two days.

Capital Double Decker & Trolley Tours

1795 BANTREE ST. • OTTAWA
(613) 749-3666 OR 1-800-823-6147 • WWW.OTTAWACAPITALTOURS.COM

C apital's fleet of trolley and double-decker buses is a real hit with kids. Capital also offers a popular after-dark tour where the guide tells spooky stories.

Gray Line
1335 CARLING AVE., SUITE #101 • OTTAWA • (613) 725-1441 OR 1-800-297-6422

G ray Line has combination excursion packages, including a bus tour-river (or canal) cruise, and a bus tour-steam train ride. There are also day-long trips that take you out of town.

☞ **SEASONS AND TIMES**
→ Capital Double Decker & Trolley Tours:
Apr—Nov, daily. Call for departure times.
Gray Line:
May—Oct, daily. Call for departure times.

☞ **COST**
→ Varies with the tour.
City tours: Adults $17 to $20, seniors and students $14 to $18, children $8 to $12. Family and group rates available.

Island Exploration on the LONG SAULT PARKWAY

BETWEEN LONG SAULT AND INGLESIDE
(613) 534-8202 OR 1-800-437-2233

T he 11 islands that make up the Long Sault Parkway were created in the late 1950s when construction of the St. Lawrence Seaway and the R. Moses-R. Saunders hydro dam caused flooding in the area. Today, 11 kilometres of scenic causeways and bridges link the islands together. This is good news for families. Several parks scattered over the islands offer sandy swimming beaches, campgrounds, nature trails, bicycle paths and picnic sites. On Mille Roches, Woodlands and McLaren islands there are also playgrounds, boat launches, sports facilities and playing fields. Visitors to Macdonell Island can take in Lost Villages, a display featuring memorabilia and photos of six villages that were flooded by the power dam project.

☞ **SEASONS AND TIMES**
➤ Parkway: Mid-May—late Sept, daily.
Campgrounds: Call for opening and closing dates.

☞ **COST**
➤ Parkway user fee: Adults $ 2.25, children under 12, bicyclists and pedestrians, free. Free parking. User fees for other activities.

☞ **GETTING THERE**
➤ By car, take Wellington St. east (its name changes to Rideau St., then Montreal Rd.) to Aviation Pkwy. and go south. Merge onto 417 E. and take Exit 58 (Rte. 138 S.) to Cornwall. Access Hwy. 401 W. and continue to Exit 778 at Long Sault. Follow the posted signs to the parkway. About one hour from Parliament Hill.

☞ **NEARBY**
➤ Upper Canada Migratory Bird Sanctuary.

☞ **COMMENT**
➤ Operated by the St. Lawrence Parks Commission. Plan a 4-hour visit.

Cool!
IT'S AN ICE BRIDGE

**BETWEEN MONTEBELLO, QUÉBEC AND LEFAIVRE, ONTARIO
(613) 679-4505**

☞ **SEASONS AND TIMES**
➤ Dec—Mar, weather dependent.

☞ **COST**
➤ $2.50 per car.

☞ **GETTING THERE**
➤ By car, take Wellington St. east (it becomes Rideau St.) to King Edward Ave. and go north over the Macdonald-Cartier Bridge to Autoroute 50 E. (it becomes Rte. 148). The ice bridge is just past Montebello—follow the ferry signs. About one hour from Parliament Hill. Returning home, from Lefaivre follow Rte. 15 south to County Rd. 174 W., formerly Hwy. 17 W., and continue to Ottawa.

Every year an ice bridge is constructed over the Ottawa River between Montebello and Lefaivre. If you're returning to the city after a day of skiing or a visit to Parc Oméga, why not use it? You'll enjoy the scenery, and when the weather is fine you may even see people ice fishing on the river.

In warmer months a ferry service operates between the two towns. But as soon as the temperature drops and the river freezes, crews begin watering the route twice daily. Cars are allowed on only when the ice is 31 centimetres thick. You may not be able to cross the river at all in late spring when the ice is too thin for cars but still too thick for the ferry to plow through. On those days you'll have to return home the way you came.

೨೨೨

Power and Speed
MACDONALD-CARTIER INTERNATIONAL AIRPORT

SOUTH END OF AIRPORT PKWY.
GLOUCESTER
(613) 248-2125

☞ **SEASONS AND TIMES**
➤ Year-round· Daily.

☞ **COST**
➤ Free. Parking extra.

☞ **GETTING THERE**
➤ By car, take Wellington St. west to Bay St. and go south. Turn west on Somerset St. to Bronson Ave. and head south. Bronson becomes the Airport Pkwy., which leads to the airport terminal. Pay parking on site. About 2o minutes from Parliament Hill.
➤ By public transit, take OC Transpo bus 96. There's also an Airport/Hotel shuttle service. Call (613) 736-9993 or 1-888-862-7433 for more information.

☞ **NEARBY**
➤ Mooney's Bay.

Most kids are fascinated by big machinery, and there's nothing bigger than an airplane. So why not take your children to the Macdonald-Cartier International Airport, where they can spend time in the observation lounge watching planes take off and land? They'll be mesmerized to see a jet hurtle down the runway, engines roaring. The nose lifts, gradually at first, then the wheels go up, and suddenly a lumbering beast is transformed into a sleek flying machine. Even the baggage trains are of interest as they zip back and forth on the tarmac. Afterward, head to the second floor of the airport, where you'll find a small play area that has building blocks and a few toys.

Going Public
TAKING CITY BUSES

OC Transpo

1500 St. Laurent Blvd. • Ottawa • (613) 741-4390 • www.octranspo.com

Société de transport de l'Outaouais (STO)

111, rue Jean-Proulx (Jean-Proulx St.) • Hull, Québec
(819) 770-3242 • www.sto.ca

Two public transit companies serve the Ottawa-Hull area. On the south side of the Ottawa River, OC Transpo operates buses in the Ottawa-Carleton region, serving the communities of Cumberland, Gloucester, Kanata, Nepean, Ottawa, Rockcliffe and Vanier. On the north side of the river, the STO provides bus transportation to Aylmer, Buckingham, Cantley, Chelsea, Gatineau, Hull and Masson-Angers in the Outaouais region. Both companies have park-and-ride lots and use reserved express lanes (these routes have higher fares), making public transit convenient, economical and worry-free.

To facilitate cross-river trips, both companies accept the other's monthly passes and transfers, but not tickets. Also, passengers have to pay a surcharge of $0.50 when switching lines ($1 on express lines, $2.50 on interzone lines). If you missed your bus, call the telephone number posted at your stop to find out when the next two buses will arrive. Route maps for OC Transpo are available at the Customer Service Centre at Place de Ville, and at the Place d'Orléans, St. Laurent and Lincoln Fields stations. STO maps are available on the buses, at the STO office and at some ticket sellers.

☞ SEASONS AND TIMES

→ Year-round: Daily, generally 6 am—1 am. Check your bus stop or call the company for details. Some routes begin operating as early as 4 am.

☞ COST

→ OC Transpo

Fares: Adult, senior and student fare, regular $2.25 or 2 tickets, express $3.50 or 3 tickets, children (6 to 11) $1.25 or 1 ticket, children under 6 free. Tickets are sold in books of 10 for $7.50. Monthly passes: Adult Unipass (all routes) $72.50, student Unipass $56.75, Adult Transpass (non-express) $57, student Transpass $46.75. Seniors' pass (all routes) $28.

Tickets and passes can be purchased at some variety stores, the Customer Service Centre at Place de Ville, and at the Place d'Orléans, St. Laurent and Lincoln Fields stations. ID cards are required when using passes.

→ STO

Fares: Adult, senior and student, regular $2.60 or 1 ticket, express $3.10 or 1 ticket plus $0.50, children under 6 free. Adult tickets are sold in books of 6 for $12, students' and seniors' tickets are sold 6 for $9.

Monthly passes: Adult Laissez-passer express $72, regular $57, seniors' pass (all routes) $26, student express pass $54, regular $42. ID cards are required when using passes and students' and seniors' tickets.

Tickets and passes can be purchased at some variety stores or at the STO office during business hours (8:30 am—noon, 1 pm—4:30 pm).

☞ COMMENT

→ Passengers must use exact change when paying cash fares. If you're not using a pass, pick up a transfer as proof of payment.

CHAPTER 11

Favourite Festivals

E verybody loves a party. From the Governor
General's Levy on New Year's Day to the
Canada Day bash on Parliament Hill, residents of Ottawa-Hull find reason to celebrate year-
round. This chapter lists the area's most popular
festivals, including the Children's Festival de la
Jeunesse, La Fête St-Jean, Le Festival franco-
ontarien and the National Capital Dragon Boat Race
Festival. Take your children to Winterlude, where
they'll play games in the snow. Or head to the
Gatineau Hot Air Balloon Festival for a balloon ride
or to the Tulip Festival for the boat parade. Some
families prefer the quiet pleasures of spending a
day with furry friends at the CHEO Teddy Bear
Picnic. If you like midway rides, music or fireworks,
check out the Central Canada Exhibition, the CKCU
Ottawa Folk Festival and the Casino Sound of Light.
For even more festivals, go to the Directory of
Events at the back of the book. Whatever your destination, festivals mean hours of affordable fun for
the whole family.

Whooping It Up at the CENTRAL CANADA EXHIBITION

LANSDOWNE PARK
1015 BANK ST.
OTTAWA
(613) 237-7222 OR **(613) 569-3998**
WWW.THE-EX.COM

The Central Canada Exhibition, or the Ex as it's affectionately called, promises families freewheeling fun and excitement over 11 days. Younger children will enjoy Kids' World with its carousel, pony ring and other pint-sized rides. Their older siblings will head straight for the midway, which has lots of adventure rides and games of chance to choose from. When hunger strikes and you need a snack or a meal, you'll find dozens of food stands on the grounds.

For a taste of rural Ontario, be certain to visit the agriculture exhibitions with their livestock shows and displays of farm produce and baked goods.

☞ **SEASONS AND TIMES**
➤ Aug 19—29, 1999, daily, 12 pm—12 am. (Opening day, 4 pm—12 am.)
Aug 17—27, 2000.
Aug 16—26, 2001.

☞ **COST**
➤ Admission: Adults and adolescents (12 to 17) $ 5.99, children (2 to 11) $ 2.99, under 2 free.
No charge after 10:30 pm.
Ride coupons $0.75. Midway bracelets (unlimited rides), $22.50 per person.

☞ **GETTING THERE**
➤ By car, take Bank St. south to Lansdowne Park. Limited pay parking ($15) on site. About 10 minutes from Parliament Hill. Some area residents will rent their driveways for less. There is also parking at Carleton University and a shuttle bus to the Ex.
➤ By public transit, take OC Transpo buses 1 or 7 (bus 11 during rush hour.)
➤ By bicycle, follow the Rideau Canal Pathway (west side) to Lansdowne Park.

You can also attend the Ex's daily spectacles, which include magic shows, juggling and fire-eating acts and animal events featuring trained tigers. Show times are posted on the billboard near the main gate. The Lost Children Centre, where you can pick up identification stickers for kids, is also there.

Up, Up and Away at GATINEAU'S BALLOON FESTIVAL

LA BAIE PARK
93, RUE ST-LOUIS (ST. LOUIS ST.), GATINEAU, QUÉBEC
(819) 243-2330 OR 1-800-668-8383
COMM@VILLE.GATINEAU.QC.CA
HTTP://WWW.VILLE.GATINEAU.QC.CA

☞ **SEASONS AND TIMES**
➤ Sept 3—6, 1999, 6 am—11 pm.

☞ **COST**
➤ Admission (shows included, midway rides extra): $15 per person, children under 120 cm free, one-day pass $12, four-day pass $20 (must be purchased before Sept. 2).
Balloon ride: $130 per person.

Anyone with a dream of sailing through the sky in a hot-air balloon can realize it here. Or maybe you're a spectator at heart. Either way, there's plenty to see and do at Gatineau's four-day ballooning festival, which also features clowns, magicians, acrobats, outdoor concerts and a fairground with rides.

To get close to the action, go to the launching area along the river front, where you'll find as many as 150 seven-storey balloons in all colours and shapes, including castles, dragons, medieval knights, trucks, rabbits and popular cartoon characters. For a truly wonderful sight, be there at 6:30 am and 6:30 pm daily, when the balloons lift off en masse (the air must be stable and the winds calm). The liftoffs are also visible from Rockcliffe Lookout, Rideau Falls Park and other spots around town. Feel like going along? A three-hour adventure includes balloon inflation, flight and return ride.

☞ **GETTING THERE**
➤ By car, take Wellington St. east (its name changes to Rideau St.) to King Edward Ave. go north and cross the Macdonald-Cartier Bridge. Take Fournier Blvd. E. to St. Louis St. in Gatineau. The park is on the right. Limited pay parking on site. Some residents rent their driveways. About 20 minutes from Parliament Hill.
➤ By public transit, take the free STO shuttle from Les Promenades de l'Outaouais mall. Call (819) 770-3242.

☞ **NEARBY**
➤ Leamy Lake Park, Rapides-Farmers Power Station.

☞ **COMMENT**
➤ Operated by the Municipality of Gatineau. Plan to spend the day.

☞ **SIMILAR ATTRACTION**
➤ **Cornwall Liftoff** (Aug 20–23). Cornwall, Ontario (613) 933-8973, or www.visit.cornwall.on.ca

A Mid-winter Break
WINTERLUDE

VARIOUS LOCATIONS THROUGHOUT OTTAWA-HULL
(613) 239-5000 OR **1-800-465-1867**
INFO@NCC-CCN.CA
WWW.CAPCAN.CA

☞ **SEASONS AND TIMES**

→ First three weekends of February, Fri—Sun, 10 am—8 pm, generally. Times vary per activity.

☞ **COST**

→ Free for most activities.

☞ **GETTING THERE**

→ Getting there is not a problem, but finding parking is. For free, easy-to-access parking, go to the Robert Guertin Arena in Hull, where you'll find a free shuttle service to Winterlude sites. Buses run regularly from the arena between 11 am and 10 pm on Fridays and Saturdays; until 5 pm on Sundays. For details, call OC Transpo (613) 741-4390 or STO (819) 770-3242. To get to the arena, go north across the Alexandra Bridge and continue north on St. Laurent Blvd. until St-Redempteur St. Go east to Allard St. Minutes from Parliament Hill.

☞ **COMMENT**

→ Operated by the National Capital Commission, the City of Ottawa and other sponsors. All of the sites are accessible to wheelchairs and strollers, though not every activity is.

You can't beat winter weather, so why not enjoy it? Come to Winterlude, which celebrates every part of Canada's most notorious season for three weekends in February. This well-loved outdoor festival attracts thousands of families to the Rideau Canal, Dow's Lake, Jacques-Cartier Park, Parliament Hill and other sites, where they skate, toboggan, go for sleigh rides, play games in the snow, admire ice sculptures and attend concerts and skating shows. The Snowflake Kingdom at Jacques-Cartier Park (page 160) organizes lots of activities for kids and is particularly popular. Or take the family skating for the afternoon at the Skateway on the Rideau Canal (page

27). At Dow's Lake, you may arrive in time to see a hot-air balloon lift off. Your day won't be complete without tasting a beaver tail, a hot, sweet pastry that hits the spot every time. If you have small children, you may want to replace your stroller with a sled.

Visit the Capital Infocentre at 90 Wellington Street to obtain a calendar that lists the times of the activities at these and other Winterlude sites, including Confederation Park, ByWard Market, the Canadian Museum of Nature, the Canadian Museum of Civilization, Gatineau Park and Sparks Street Mall.

Other Favourite Festivals

The Canadian Tulip Festival

MAJOR'S HILL PARK AND OTHER LOCATIONS IN OTTAWA-HULL
(613) 567-5757 (OTTAWA) OR (819) 595-7400 (HULL)
WWW.TULIPFESTIVAL.CA
WWW.VILLE.HULL.QC.CA/TOURISME/FESTTULIPE.HTM

This 11-day floral extravaganza, which is the largest tulip festival in the world, has plenty of activities for families. Most of the action is centred at Major's Hill Park (page 172), where music, song and dance are performed on four stages. The park also has a Tulip Craft Fair, an International Village featuring food concessions and a family area where kids can have their faces painted. Festivities are also held at 12 other sites. Always popular with kids are the fireworks on Carnival Night and the Parade on Water, a flotilla of 60 boats that sails from Dow's Lake to Parliament Hill on the Rideau Canal. There are also beautiful tulip displays at Commissioners Park, and the Maison du Citoyen in Hull features the Salon de la gastronomie outaouaise. There is a shuttle service.

☞ May 14 to 24, 1999 · May 12 to 22, 2000.

☞ Major's Hill Park: Free before 5 pm on weekdays. After 5 pm and on weekends, $10 per person, $5 per person for groups, children 12 and under free.

☞ Take Wellington St. east to Mackenzie Ave. and go north. Minutes from Parliament Hill.

Children's Festival de la Jeunesse

CANADIAN MUSEUM OF NATURE • 240 MCLEOD ST. • OTTAWA
(613) 728-5863 • WWW.CHILDFEST.CA

This unique festival provides children with excellent and affordable theatrical entertainment in French and English. The five-day event boasts 80 performances by mainly Canadian artists, and many of the shows encourage audience participation. The ticket price includes admission to the museum and entrance to the craft tent and several activities. In the fall and winter you can subscribe to a series that offers plays, concerts, puppet shows and a Christmas pantomime. Tickets to individual shows are available.

☞ Festival: First week of June. Call for dates.
Fall-winter season: Oct–Apr.
Pantomime: Dec 26 to 31.

☞ Festival tickets: $6 per show per person; groups, $5 per show ($4.50 if bought before Mar 1); activities only, $3.50.

☞ Fall-winter season: Subscription, $54. Prices vary for individual shows.

☞ Take Elgin St. south to McLeod St. and go west for one block. Take OC Transpo buses 5, 6, 14 or 99.

Festival franco-ontarien
FESTIVAL PLAZA • LAURIER AVE. AND ELGIN ST. • OTTAWA • (613) 741-1225

This week-long celebration of French culture is one of the biggest in North America, hosting French-speaking performers from the Ottawa-Hull area and from across Canada and around the world. It's a great chance to see the Francophonie in action. You don't have to understand French to enjoy the concerts at such venues as the Astrolabe Theatre, or the street performers, and your kids will love the party-like atmosphere. Some of the shows will be broadcast by Radio-Canada.

☞ June 22 to 27, 1999.
June 20 to 25, 2000.

☞ Tickets start at $11 per day.
Free shows at ByWard Market and the National Gallery of Canada.

La Fête St-Jean
(819) 595-7400 (HULL) • (819) 684-7119 (AYLMER)

La Fête St-Jean (Feast of St. John the Baptist), which falls on June 24, is a celebration of Québécois culture and traditions. When it comes to this historic date, francophones on both sides of the Ottawa River show they know how to throw a good party. Parc Mousette on de Lanaudière Street in Hull is the best place for families to enjoy the celebration, where activities include face-painting, organized games, live music, a picnic and a roaring bonfire in the evening. The park has a swimming beach and nature trails, so if the weather's fine, pack your swimsuits and plan to make a day of it. Most municipalities in Québec mark the holiday with parties that feature parades, family entertainment and special activities for kids. There's a rundown of the festivities in the Directory of Events. Also, check under Fête St-Jean in the General Index.

☞ June 24, all day.

☞ Free for most activities.

National Capital Dragon Boat Race Festival

RIDEAU CANOE CLUB • HOG'S BACK RD. NEAR MOONEY'S BAY • OTTAWA
(613) 238-7711 • WWW.DRAGONBOAT.NET

Combine fantastical creatures with water and speed, throw in food and entertainment, and you've got a great way to spend a summer day with your family. Everyone will be captivated as the teams of 22 men and women furiously paddle their dragon-shaped craft toward the finish line to the cheers of the crowd. After the races, you can take in live shows and enjoy a picnic beside the Rideau River. Corporations and non-profit groups are welcome to enter racing teams. Entry fees help fund the festival. For details, check out the Web site.

☞ June 26 to 27, 1999. The races are usually held the last weekend in June or the first weekend in July.

☞ Outdoor events are free.

☞ Take Bronson Ave. south to Heron Rd. and go west to Riverside Dr. Turn south to Hog's Back Rd.

Canada Day

VARIOUS LOCATIONS AROUND TOWN
(613) 239-5000 OR 1-800-465-1867 • WWW.CAPCAN.CA

July 1 is Canada's birthday, and Ottawa is party central. Begin the day-long celebrations by attending the morning parade, which marches from the Supreme Court building to Parliament Hill, where there is a flag-raising ceremony. Afterward, you can watch the Changing of the Guard, listen to marching bands and see live entertainment performed throughout the day. Don't miss the spectacular fireworks display in the evening. But the party isn't confined to the Hill. There are concerts, games, face-painting and crafts for kids, refreshments and other events at Major's Hill Park, Confederation Park, Jacques-Cartier Park and the World Exchange Plaza Terrace. It's also a good day for a museum visit. Most federally operated museums offer free admission on Canada Day, and some have special activities for families. You can obtain a free Canada Day schedule of events at the Capital Infocentre at 90 Wellington Street.

Many municipalities in the area host Canada Day parties. Some of the activities are listed in the Directory of Events. Also, check under Canada Day in the General Index.

☞   July 1, all day.

☞   Free for most activities.

Children's Hospital of Eastern Ontario (CHEO) Teddy Bear Picnic
RIDEAU HALL • 1 SUSSEX DR. • OTTAWA • (613) 737-2780

The spacious grounds of Rideau Hall are filled with teddy bears and their friends at this annual event for families. The day is packed with activities that kick off at 8 am with a pancake breakfast that's served by local celebrities. Kids can bring their injured teddies to the B*A*S*H Tent for some TLC, watch a parade, cuddle the animals at the petting zoo and meet a Mountie. They'll also enjoy the free midway rides, organized games and live entertainment.

☞ The picnic is held on the second Saturday in July.
July 10, 1999.
July 8, 2000.

☞ Admission and activities are free (donations are appreciated). You pay for your food.

☞ Take Wellington St. east to Sussex Dr. and go north. Rideau Hall is just beyond the Rideau River.
Take OC Transpo bus 3.

The Casino Sound of Light
LEAMY LAKE • HULL, QUÉBEC
(819) 771-3389 OR 1-888-429-3389
HTTP://WWW.VILLE.HULL.QC.CA/TOURISME/GRANDFEUX.HTM

Who doesn't love fireworks? This international pyrotechnics competition, which is held over three Saturday nights and two Wednesday nights, lights up the evening skies over Leamy Lake. Music accompanies the show. Bring your own lawn chairs or blankets. Toilets are available.

☞ July 31 and Aug 4, 7, 11 and 14, 1999.

☞ Reserved seating: $16 per person on competition nights;
$20 for the grand finale.
General admission: Adults $8, children under 12 free.

☞ Take the Macdonald-Cartier Bridge and access Rte. 148 E.
Continue across the Leamy Creek Bridge and take
the first exit south.

CKCU Ottawa Folk Festival

BRITANNIA PARK • CARLING AVE. AND PINECREST RD. • OTTAWA
(613) 230-8234 • WWW.OTTAWAFOLK.ORG

O utdoor folk festivals are joyous occasions and
perfect venues for family entertainment, where
you and your kids can enjoy every flavour of folk
music, from fiddle to rock. This festival also offers
interactive workshops, a craft village and a Family
Area, where kids can have their faces painted, watch
children's entertainers and play organized games.
Some performers lead sing-alongs, others teach children how to make musical instruments. There's also a
reading tent sponsored by *The Ottawa Citizen*. Leave
your pets and tape recorders at home.

☞ Last weekend in August.

☞ While other prices for 1999 were unavailable at printing time,
the Early Bird Pass will be under $25.

☞ Take Wellington St. west to the Ottawa River Pkwy.
and continue to Britannia Park.
Take OC Transpo buses 2, 18, 85, 97, 171 or 172.

CHAPTER 12

FARTHER AFIELD

While this guide was designed to provide you with a variety of fun outings in the National Capital Region, a few sites that are a bit farther afield couldn't be left out. At Prehistoric World in Morrisburg, your kids can come face-to-face with all their favourite dinosaurs. While you're in the neighbourhood, visit the Upper Canada Bird Sanctuary or Upper Canada Village. If you want to see live animals, take the gang to Parc Oméga in Montebello. Or make the chocolate-lovers in your family happy with a visit to the Hershey's plant in Smiths Falls. At the same time you can check out the Smiths Falls Railway Museum and the Rideau Canal Museum, which are nearby. Other out-of-town destinations include Le Château Montebello, Mikey's Fun Factory, the Native North American Travelling College Museum, the Nor'Westers and Loyalists Museum and the St. Lawrence-FDR Power Project. While all these sites fall outside the guide's "one-hour rule" for travel, after reading about them, you'll agree that they're worth the drive to get to.

Life in the 1860s at UPPER CANADA VILLAGE

COUNTY RD. 2
MORRISBURG
(613) 543-3704 OR 1-800-437-2233
GETAWAY@PARKS.ON.CA
WWW.PARKS.ON.CA

I f you're looking for charm and pioneer authenticity, come to Upper Canada Village, where both are provided in abundance. About 50 heritage buildings are spread out over 27 hectares, re-creating a rural community of the 1860s. Visit beautifully maintained homes, farmsteads, churches, a schoolhouse, a blacksmith's shop, a flour mill, a tavern, a general store and much more. Actors dressed in period costumes are on hand at every turn, sowing seeds with the help of oxen or weaving or working the printing press. Full of interesting information about the times and the village, they'll chat with you in 19th-century vernacular.

Visitors may join guided bilingual tours or stroll the grounds on their own. If you tire of walking, hop aboard the horse-drawn

🖙 **SEASONS AND TIMES**
➤ Victoria Day—Thanksgiving, daily, 9:30 am—5 pm.

🖙 **COST**
➤ Adults $12.95, children (5 to 12) $ 6.25, under 4 free, families receive a 10% discount.

🖙 **GETTING THERE**
➤ By car, take Bank St. south (it becomes County Rd. 31, formerly Hwy. 31) to Morrisburg, then follow County Rd. 2 (formerly Hwy. 2) east about 10 kilometres to the village. It's on the right. Free parking on site. About one hour from Parliament Hill.
➤ By bus, Gray Line has a Thousand Islands cruise that includes an Upper Canada Village tour. Call (613) 725-3047.

☞ **NEARBY**
➤ Prehistoric World, Crysler Beach, Crysler Farm, Queen Elizabeth Flower Gardens.

☞ **COMMENT**
➤ Operated by the St. Lawrence Parks Commission. Diaper-changing facilities. Plan to spend the day.

wagon that circles the village at regular intervals. After so much looking and listening, children will be impatient to reach the activity centre, which has period games and toys for them to play with and costumes to try on. They'll also love climbing to the top of the lookout for a view of the St. Lawrence River on one side and the town on the other. Afterward, take the miniature train to Crysler Beach, which departs regularly from its station just outside the main gate. You'll find picnic tables and a sandy swimming beach.

There are live-in adventures for children eight and older who are interested in staying in the village overnight. They are provided with accommodation, and will perform chores in the community.

Close Encounters with Dinosaurs at PREHISTORIC WORLD

UPPER CANADA ROAD
MORRISBURG, ONTARIO
(613) 543-2503

It's one thing to read about dinosaurs, it's quite another to see them up close in a primeval forest. Prehistoric World has faithfully reproduced 50 dinosaurs and other prehistoric beasts in life-size, including a stegosaurus, a tyrannosaurus, a woolly mammoth and a triceratops. Placed strategically along a concrete trail that winds through the park, each dinosaur is accompanied by a panel containing bilingual biographical information. The setting is incredibly authentic-looking, with ferns growing abundantly on the forest floor.

Composed of a metal frame covered with concrete and then painted, each dinosaur requires about five months to complete. It's likely that during your visit you'll spot some under construction. But unlike Hollywood's reproductions, these ones don't attack. In fact, they don't even move. All of Prehistoric World's exhibits are stationary.

Some kids will like digging for fossils in the park's sandy "paleontology" pit, while others will be content running around the adjacent large, grassy field. Tables have been provided for picnicking. A nearby restaurant offers take-out.

☞ **SEASONS AND TIMES**
➤ May 23—Labour Day, daily, 10 am—4 pm.
Group visits possible at other times.

☞ **COST**
➤ Adults $6, children $4.25, under 4 free.
Group rates available.

☞ **GETTING THERE**
➤ By car, take Bank St. south (it becomes County Rd. 31, formerly Hwy. 31) to Hwy. 401 E. Take Exit 758, go south and follow the posted dinosaur signs. Free parking on site. About one hour from Parliament Hill.

☞ **NEARBY**
➤ Upper Canada Village, Upper Canada Bird Sanctuary.

☞ **COMMENT**
➤ The concrete path is bumpy. Plan a 1-hour visit.

An Illuminating Visit
ST. LAWRENCE-FDR POWER PROJECT VISITORS CENTRE

RTE. 131 N. MASSENA, NEW YORK
(315) 764-0226
WWW.NYPA.GOV/HTML/VCSTLAWR.HTML

☞ **SEASONS AND TIMES**
➤ Summer: Late May—Sept, daily, 9 am—6 pm.
Winter: Oct—late May, Mon—Fri, 9 am—4:30 pm.

☞ **COST**
➤ Free.

☞ **GETTING THERE**
➤ By car, take Wellington St. east (its name will change to Rideau St., then Montreal Rd.) to Aviation Pkwy. and turn south. Merge onto Hwy. 417 E. and take Exit 58 (Rte. 138 S.) to Cornwall. Follow Brookdale Ave. to the toll bridge to New York State, then access Rte. 37 W. to Massena. Turn north on Rte. 131 and follow the signs to the centre. Free parking on site. About 90 minutes from Parliament Hill.

☞ **NEARBY**
➤ Eisenhower Lock, R. Moses State Park.

☞ **COMMENT**
➤ Operated by the New York Power Authority. Diaper-changing facilities. Plan a 2-hour visit.

Located beside the R. Moses-R. Saunders hydro dam, this energy centre has three floors of interactive exhibits and computer games that demonstrate how electricity is made and used. Children will get a charge out of pedalling the bicycle generator and watching the lights go on. There is a working model of the dam and displays about energy conservation. An observation deck outside offers spectacular views of the dam, which spans the U.S.-Canadian border (tours are offered), and of the St. Lawrence River and Adirondack Mountains. Younger children won't learn as much about electricity as their older siblings will, but they'll be happy pushing buttons.

You can find vending machines on site. For something more substantial, restaurants and a shopping mall are located nearby. In fair weather you may want to picnic at the Eisenhower Lock, just five minutes away on Rte. 131.

Decidedly Delicious HERSHEY'S CHOCOLATE FACTORY

1 HERSHEY DR.
SMITHS FALLS
(613) 283-3300
WWW.TOWN.SMITHS-FALLS.ON.CA

This is your chance to see how chocolate bars are made. From the elevated deck of the Visitors Centre you'll have a bird's-eye view of the production line below, where your favourite chocolate treats are taking shape (weekdays only). The self-guided tours are made easier by bilingual panels that describe the candy-making process. The Heritage Room has photographs and a video that detail the history of the company.

Your tour won't be complete without a visit to the gift shop, where the Hershey product

---

☞ **SEASONS AND TIMES**
➤ Year-round: Mon—Fri, 9 am— 6 pm; Sat, 9 am—5 pm; Sun, 10 am— 4 pm.
The production line is closed on weekends. Call ahead for holiday closures.

☞ **COST**
➤ Tour: Free.

line, including cut-cost factory rejects, are available for purchase. Free samples are sometimes available at the cash. To avoid a chocolaty mess on warm-weather days, bring a cooler to transport your acquisitions home.

☞ **GETTING THERE**

➺ By car, take O'Connor St. south to Laurier Ave. and go west. Turn south on Bronson Ave. to access Hwy. 16 S. At Kemptville take County Rd. 43 W. (formerly Hwy. 43) to Smiths Falls. The factory is visible on the right shortly after entering town. Free parking on site. About 75 minutes from Parliament Hill.

➺ Via Rail runs a return train every day except on Saturday between Ottawa and Smiths Falls. For price and departure information, call 1-888-842-7733. The plant is a 15-minute walk from the station, or bring your bicycles and tour Smiths Falls afterward. There is a free shuttle bus on summer weekends. Call 1-800-257-1334 for details.

☞ **NEARBY**

➺ Rideau Canal Museum, Heritage House Museum, Smiths Falls Railway Museum.

☞ **COMMENT**

➺ Plan a 1-hour visit.

Going on Safari at
PARC OMÉGA

399 ROUTE 323 N.
MONTEBELLO, QUÉBEC
(819) 423-5487 OR 1-888-423-5487
INFO@PARC-OMEGA.COM
WWW.PARC.OMEGA.COM

Before beginning your tour it would be prudent to purchase a $1 bag of carrots at the main gate. They'll come in handy when you meet up with the park's perpetually hungry elk and deer. But don't leave your car to feed them. Other creatures, some quite fierce, also roam the 600 hectares of the reserve. These include wild boar, bison, moose, timber wolves, black bears and coyotes. For safety, visitors are asked to stay in their cars for the entire 10-kilometre drive. But you won't be alone—by tuning your radio to FM 88.1, you can hear commentary about the animals provided by the park.

Parc Oméga also has two short hiking trails and an exhibit of birds of prey. An on-site restaurant serves full meals, or relax at the outdoor picnic area. Guided tours are usually provided to groups only, however,

☞ **SEASONS AND TIMES**
➤ Year-round: Daily, 10 am—4:30 pm.

☞ **COST**
➤ July 1—Sept 7: Adults $12, children (6 to 15) $6, tots (2 to 5) $2. Other times: Adults $9, children (6 to 15) $4.50, under 6 free. Group rates available.

☞ **GETTING THERE**
➤ By car, take Wellington St. east (its name changes to Rideau St.) to King Edward Ave. and go north over the Macdonald-Cartier Bridge to Autoroute 50 E. (it becomes Rte. 148). Continue to Rte. 323 N. in Montebello and go north for about three kilometres. The park is on the left. Free parking on site. About one hour from Parliament Hill.

☞ **NEARBY**
➤ Château Montebello, Manoir Papineau, Plaisance Cheese Factory, Plaisance Wetlands Park.

☞ **COMMENT**
➤ Privately run. Bilingual staff. The hiking trails are not accessible to wheelchairs or strollers. Plan a 3-hour visit.

personal tours are available if you make prior arrangements with park staff. Don't forget your binoculars.

Steering Your Course at the RIDEAU CANAL MUSEUM

34 BECKWITH ST. S.
SMITHS FALLS
(613) 284-0505
WWW.TOWN.SMITHS-FALLS.ON.CA

☞ **SEASONS AND TIMES**
➤ May 24–Thanksgiving, daily,
9 am–5 pm.

☞ **COST**
➤ Adults, $2.50, seniors $2.25, students $2, children (6 to 12) $1.50, families $7.

☞ **GETTING THERE**
➤ By car, take O'Connor St. south to Laurier Ave. and turn west. At Bronson Ave. go south and access Hwy. 16 S. to Kemptville. Take County Rd. 43 W. (formerly Hwy. 43) to Smiths Falls and turn south on Beckwith St. The museum is on the right. Free parking on site. About 75 minutes from Parliament Hill.
➤ Via Rail operates a train from Ottawa to Smith Falls (page 228).

☞ **NEARBY**
➤ Hershey Chocolate Factory, Smiths Falls Railway Museum, Heritage House Museum.

☞ **COMMENT**
➤ Plan a 1-hour visit.

☞ **SIMILAR ATTRACTION**
➤ **Bytown Museum**, near the Ottawa Locks, Ottawa (613) 234-4570.

There's lots for children to do at this museum, starting with climbing to the top of the indoor observation tower to view the canal and the pretty town of Smiths Falls. That done, it's time to explore the four floors of exhibits. Kids will especially enjoy steering a virtual boat at the Canal Captain exhibit, inspecting a giant model of the canal and taking in laser-disk and video presentations, which can be found on every floor.

Located in the historic stone buildings of Woods Mill constructed in the 1880s, the museum also has displays about the canal's history and construction including an extensive collection of 19th-century tools its builders used to complete the project. Touch-screen computers located throughout the museum feature games and quizzes that will test kids' knowledge of such subjects as Ottawa Valley history and geography, and there are preserved and poster exhibits of wildlife that inhabit the waterway.

If your kids become restless, a nearby municipal park has a playground and picnic tables, as well as telephones and an information centre.

Bird-watching at the UPPER CANADA MIGRATORY BIRD SANCTUARY

INGLESIDE
1-800-437-2233
WWW.PARKS.ON.CA

This is a good place to introduce children to nature. Hugging the banks of the St. Lawrence River southwest of Cornwall, the sanctuary's 1,400 hectares of forests and wetlands are an important stopover for nearly 150 bird species that use the Atlantic flyway to reach nesting and wintering grounds, including Canada geese, mallards and wood ducks. The area is also populated by black bear, moose, turtles and other creatures.

☞ **SEASONS AND TIMES**
➤ May 15—late Oct, daily, 8:30 am—
4:30 pm.

☞ **COST**
➤ Free. (Donations appreciated.)
Program fees: $2.50 per person.

☞ **GETTING THERE**
➤ By car, take Bank St. south. It
becomes County Rd. 31 (formerly
Hwy. 31). Drive to Morrisburg, then
follow County Rd. 2 E. (formerly
Hwy. 2) and look for the bird sanctuary on your right. Free parking on
site. About 90 minutes from
Parliament Hill.

☞ **COMMENT**
➤ Diaper-changing facilities. Plan a
3-hour visit.

The whole family will enjoy the self-guided nature walks. You'll learn about biodiversity and conservation as you follow the eight kilometres of rustic hiking trails, complete with small bridges and boardwalks. Your children will be eager to climb to the top of the observation tower, where they'll get a bird's eye view of the sanctuary. At the interpretive centre you'll find taxidermal specimens and animal skeletons that can be touched, as well as various colouring activities.

The sanctuary offers regular events, including guided tours and goose-feeding demonstrations (Sept 15—late Oct, daily, 2:30 pm). There are also family campouts and educational nature programs for youth. To obtain a copy of the sanctuary's calendar of events, call 1-800-437-2233 or visit its Web site.

The Native North American TRAVELLING COLLEGE MUSEUM

RR #3 (THE EAST END)
CORNWALL ISLAND
(613) 932-9452

At the heart of this museum, which offers visitors a history of three First Nations peoples—the Cree, the Ojibwe and the Iroquois—is the village, a faithful reproduction of an early 1600s Iroquois settlement. The whole family will want to explore the wooden stockade, the longhouse, the sweat lodge and the arbour, where songs and dances are performed during Friendship Days (in early July).

Inside the small museum building are exhibits of artifacts. While there are few explanatory panels and no interactive displays, friendly tour guides will tell you about the collection's significance and will invite the children to touch some of the pieces, which include traditional costumes, turtle rattles, wampum, weapons and a remarkable sketch on deer skin about Iroquois Confederacy history.

☞ **SEASONS AND TIMES**
➤ Year-round: Mon—Fri, 8 am—noon and 1 pm—4 pm.
Open weekends during special events.

☞ **COST**
➤ Adults $3, children $1.
Toll: $4.50 per car (round trip).

☞ **GETTING THERE**
➤ By car, take Wellington St. east (its name will change to Rideau St., then Montreal Rd.) to Aviation Pkwy. and turn south. Merge onto Hwy. 417 E. and take Exit 58 (Hwy. 138 S.) to Cornwall. Follow Brookdale Ave. toward the bridge to New York State, but exit on Cornwall Island. After the toll booth, drive east for about a kilometre. The museum is on your right. Free parking on site. About 75 minutes from Parliament Hill.

The gift shop features, among other things, children's books about native culture. Bring insect repellent and dress warmly on cool days, as the museum is beside the seaway.

☞ **NEARBY**
➤ Mikey's Fun Factory, Triple D Emu Ranch, Eisenhower Lock, St. Lawrence-FDR Power Project.

☞ **COMMENT**
➤ English and Mohawk spoken. Operated by the Mohawk Nation. Plan a 1-hour visit.

☞ **SIMILAR ATTRACTION**
➤ **Akwesasne Museum and Library.** Exhibits of clothing, wampum and lacrosse are complemented by a library of native culture. Rte. 37, Hogansburg, New York (518) 358-2461.

❧❧❧

Riding the Rails at the SMITHS FALLS RAILWAY MUSEUM

90 WILLIAM ST.
SMITHS FALLS
(613) 283-5696
WWW.MAGMA.CA/~SFRM

Visitors will experience an important part of Canada's railway heritage at this museum. Situated in the town's historic 1914 Canadian Northern Railway station, the museum boasts steam and diesel locomotives, cabooses, passenger coaches and other rolling stock. Everyone is welcome to climb aboard to inspect the cars first-hand.

For children, the highlight of their visit will be pumping a handcar along a stretch of track or taking a short ride aboard a Wickham track inspection car. The whole family will enjoy the displays of model railroads. One exhibit reproduces a telegraph office. You can also view collections of old railway tools, photographs and prints, or visit the library, which includes an archives.

Besides offering tours and educational programs to schools, the museum hosts special events such as the Jigger Festival (early August), which features a parade of track cars.

☞ SEASONS AND TIMES

→ May—June 26, weekends, 10 am—4pm.
June 27—Aug 27, daily, 10 am—4 pm.
Sept—Oct, weekends, 10 am—4 pm. Call ahead, the hours are subject to change.

☞ COST

→ Adults $4, seniors and students $2.50, children under 12 free. Group rates and memberships available.

☞ GETTING THERE

→ By car, take O'Connor St. south and follow the signs for Hwy. 417 W. At Exit 132 take Hwy. 416 S. to Exit 34 (Kemptville). Take County Rd. 43 W. (formerly Hwy. 43) to Smiths Falls and turn south onto William St. (at the Ultramar gas station). The museum is on the left. Free parking on site. About 75 minutes from Parliament Hill.
→ Via Rail operates a train from Ottawa to Smith Falls (page 228).

☞ NEARBY

→ Rideau Canal Museum, Hershey Chocolate Factory, Heritage House Museum.

☞ COMMENT

→ Operated by the Smiths Falls Railway Museum Association. Only the station is accessible to wheelchairs and strollers. Plan a 1-hour visit.

Let the Good Times Roll at MIKEY'S FUN FACTORY

1020 MONTREAL RD.
CORNWALL
(613) 938-1619

☞ **SEASONS AND TIMES**
➤ Year-round: Daily, 11 am—10 pm.

☞ **COST**
➤ Mini-golf: Adults $5, children
(5 to 12) $4, 4 and under free.
Half-price on Wednesdays.
All other activities are coin-operated.

☞ **GETTING THERE**
➤ By car, take Wellington St. east (its
name will change to Rideau St., then
Montreal Rd.) to Aviation Pkwy. and
turn south. Merge onto 417 E. and
take Exit 58 (Hwy. 138 S.) to Cornwall.
Follow Brookdale Ave. south and turn
east onto Water St. (its name changes
to Montreal Rd.) and continue to the
warehouse. It's on the left. Free parking on site. About 75 minutes from
Parliament Hill.

☞ **NEARBY**
➤ Native North American Travelling
College Museum, Eisenhower Lock,
St. Lawrence-FDR Power Project.

☞ **COMMENT**
➤ Privately operated. Smoke-free.
Plan a 1-hour visit.

If your kids are clam-ouring for pure una-dulterated fun, this indoor amusement centre is the place to go. It also makes a perfect side trip after a visit to the nearby Native North American Travelling College Mu-seum (page 233). Mikey's Fun Factory is a warehouse full of games. There are batting cages, pool tables, a video arcade and a mini-golf course complete with a waterfall, a haunted house and a loop-the-loop tire.

You may want to reserve the party room for your child's birthday cele-bration. Several birthday packages are available. One even includes a clown who specializes in face-paint-ing and in organizing games for the children.

Living It Up at
LE CHÂTEAU MONTEBELLO

392, RUE NOTRE DAME (NOTRE DAME ST.)
MONTEBELLO, QUÉBEC
(819) 423-6341 OR 1-800-268-9420
WWW.CPHOTELS.CA

S ometimes it's easier to organize a family day trip if you know you're heading to luxurious surroundings. That's what you'll get at Le Château Montebello, which is a four-star all-season resort hotel. Constructed in 1930 from 10,000 red cedar logs, it offers overnight guests year-round and seasonal activities, some of which are available to the public for a fee. In the winter, bundle up your kids and test your stamina on 27 kilometres of cross-country ski trails, go ice fishing or snowshoeing, or take a ride in a horse-drawn sleigh. Snow tubing is nearby.

In summertime, you can canoe on Lac Poisson Blanc or try your luck fishing. An assortment of

☞ **SEASONS AND TIMES**
➻ Year-round: Daily.

☞ **COST**
➻ These services are available to hotel guests for no charge.
Fitness centre (per day): Adults $8, children $4.
Cross-country skiing and snowshoeing: $6 per person.
Ice fishing (per day): $10.
Horseback riding (per hour): $23.
Guided nature walks: Adults $12, children $3.
Day care per half day (1, 2 or 3 children): $12, $20 or $24.

☞ **GETTING THERE**
➻ By car, take Wellington St. east (it becomes Rideau St.) to King Edward Ave. and go north across the Macdonald-Cartier Bridge. Access Autoroute 50 E. (it becomes Rte. 148 E.) and continue to Montebello. Turn south at the first traffic light in Montebello into the hotel grounds. Free parking on site. About one hour from Parliament Hill.

☞ **NEARBY**
➤ Manoir-Papineau National
Historic Site (closed in 1999), Parc
Oméga.

☞ **COMMENT**
➤ Operated by Canadian Pacific Hotels.

watercraft can be rented. Horseback riding and guided nature walks are also offered. The fitness centre is open year-round and features an indoor pool, saunas and a whirlpool. There are indoor courts for tennis and squash. A day-care service is available.

Stepping into History at the NOR'WESTERS AND LOYALISTS MUSEUM

19651 JOHN ST.
WILLIAMSTOWN
(613) 347-3547

The mainly narrative displays in this two-room museum provide visitors with comprehensive histories of the United Empire Loyalists and the North West Company—a Montreal fur-trading company of the late 1700s. Your self-guided tour will begin in the Nor'Wester Room, where there are exhibits about the fur trade and David Thompson, who was a partner in the North West Company. Thompson explored vast areas of western Canada between 1785 and 1815. You'll see his clothing, furnishings and replicas of maps he drew. There are also animal pelts, a reproduction of a voyageur's birchbark canoe, fire bags, snowshoes and other items fur traders used on their expeditions.

Upstairs the museum has exhibits about the United Empire Loyalists, American settlers who wished to remain British subjects and came to this area after the American War for Independence. On display are military uniforms, swords, muskets, children's toys and other items from the era.

Youngsters from 6 to 10 are invited to attend the museum's week-long history program in mid-August. Every day children are treated to two hours of storytelling, plays and activities that teach them about the Loyalists and David Thompson.

☞ **SEASONS AND TIMES**
→ Summer: Mid-May–Labour Day, Sun–Fri, 1 pm–5 pm; Sat, 10 am–5 pm.
Fall: Labour Day–mid-Oct, Sat, 10 am–5 pm; Sun, 1 pm–5 pm.

☞ **COST**
→ Adults $2, seniors $2, children under 12 free.

☞ **GETTING THERE**
→ By car, take O'Connor St. south to Isabella St. and access Hwy. 417 E. Take Exit 35 to Rte. 34 S. toward Lancaster. At Rte. 17 turn west and follow the posted signs to the museum (beside the Williamstown fairgrounds). Free parking on site. About 75 minutes from Parliament Hill.

☞ **COMMENT**
→ Operated by the Glengarry Historical Society. Only the main floor is accessible to wheelchairs. Plan a 2-hour visit.

12 Months of Fun!
DIRECTORY OF EVENTS

JANUARY

January 1
Governor General's Levy
Rideau Hall, Ottawa
(613) 998-7113
1 800-465-6890

January 2, 2000
January 7, 2001
Ski-Fest
Gatineau Park
Cross-country ski fun for the
whole family
(819) 827-2020
1-800-465-1867

To January 3
Christmas Lights Across Canada
Parliament Hill and
Confederation Boulevard
(613) 239-5000
1-800-465-1867

January 25-30, 2000
Canadian Special Olympics
Various venues around Ottawa
(613) 783-3332

FEBRUARY

February 2-6, 2000
2001 dates to be announced
Ottawa-Hull International Auto
Show
Ottawa Congress Centre
1-888-311-1883

**February 4-6, 11-13, 18-20,
2000**
**February 2-4, 9-11, 16-18,
2001**
Winterlude/Bal de Neige
Downtown Ottawa-Hull, Dow's
Lake, Jacques-Cartier Park
(613) 239-5000
1-800-465-1867

February 5-14, 2000
February 3-12, 2001
Aylmer Winter Carnival
Aylmer
(819) 685-5035

February 12-13, 2000
February 10-11, 2001
Canadian Ski Marathon
Lachute to Buckingham
(819) 770-6556

February 17-20, 2000
February 15-18, 2001
Keskinada Loppet
Gatineau Park
Cross-country skiing race
(819) 827-4641
1-800-465-1867

Maple sugar time

MARCH

Mid-March
Spring Fest
Gatineau Park
Spring skiing family day
(819) 827-2020
1-800-465-1867

March 22-26, 2000
March 21-25, 2001
Salon du livre, Hull (Hull Book Fair)
Palais des congrès, Hull
(819) 243-2822

Maple sugar time

Mount Pakenham Spring Carnival
Family fun on the ski slopes
Mount Pakenham
(613) 624-5290

APRIL
April 23, 2000
April 15, 2001
Easter Egg Adventure
Fulton's Pancake House & Sugar Bush, Pakenham
(613) 256-3867

April 23, 2000
April 15, 2001
Easter Egg Hunt
Agriculture Museum, Ottawa
(613) 991-3044

MAY
May 8-9, 1999
May 13-14, 2000
National Capital Race Weekend
Festival Plaza
2 km to 42 km runs for breast cancer
(613) 237-5150 information
(613) 234-2221 tickets

May 14-24, 1999
May 12-22, 2000
Canadian Tulip Festival
Major's Hill Park, Confederation Park and Dow's Lake (613) 567-5757
(819) 595-7400 Hull events
1-800-465-1867

May 15, 1999
2000 date to be announced
Kiwanis Duck Race for Tiny Hearts, Ottawa
(613) 733-3300

May 20-25, 1999
2000 dates to be announced
Ottawa Canadian Youth Orchestra Festival
Various venues around Ottawa
(613) 234-3360

May 22-24, 1999
May 20-22, 2000
Sheep Shearing Festival
Agriculture Museum, Ottawa
(613) 991-3044

May 23-24, 1999
May 21-22, 2000
Queen Victoria's Birthday Celebrations
Upper Canada Village, Morrisburg
1-800-437-2233

May 27-30, 1999
2000 dates to be announced
Canadian Sunset Ceremony
RCMP Stables, Ottawa
(613) 993-3751

May 28-30, 1999
May 26-28, 2000
Sheepshearing Weekend
Upper Canada Village, Morrisburg
1-800-437-2233

May 29-30, 1999
2000 dates to be announced
National Capital Air Show
Macdonald-Cartier International Airport, Gloucester
(613) 526-1030

May 29-30, 1999
May 27-28, 2000
Heritage Festival
Antique vehicles, machines and
engines
Cumberland Heritage Village
Museum, Cumberland
(613) 833-3059

JUNE
June 2-6, 1999
2000 dates to be announced
Children's Festival de la
Jeunesse
Canadian Museum of Nature,
Ottawa
(613) 728-5863

June 4-12, 1999
Anne of Green Gables
Orpheus Musical Theatre
Society
Centrepoint Theatre, Ottawa
(613) 727-6650

June 9-17, 2000
Canada Dance Festival
National Arts Centre, Ottawa
(613) 996-5051

June 11-20, 1999
June 9-18, 2000
Italian Week Festival
Preston St., Ottawa
(613) 224-4388 · 726-0920

June 18-27, 1999
2000 dates to be announced
Ottawa Fringe Festival
Arts Court and Strathcona Park,
Ottawa
(613) 232-6162

June 19-20, 1999
June 17-18, 2000
Nepean Days
Andrew Haydon Park, Nepean
(613) 727-6641

June 21
National Aboriginal Day
Rideau Hall, Canadian Museum
of Civilization and National
Aviation Museum
www.aboriginalday.com

June 22-27, 1999
June 20-25, 2000
Festival franco-ontarien
Festival Plaza, Ottawa
(613) 741-1225

June 24
Fête St-Jean
Various venues in the National
Capital Region
(819) 595-7400 Hull
(819) 684-7119 Aylmer
(613) 833-3059 Cumberland
Heritage Village Museum

June 25-27, 1999
2000 dates to be announced
Strawberry Moon: A
Midsummer Festival
Saunders Farm, Munster
(613) 838-5440

June 25-27, 1999
June 23-23, 2000
Carnival of Cultures
Astrolabe Theatre, Ottawa
(613) 742-6553

June 26, 1999
(rain date June 27)
June 24, 2000
(rain date June 25)
Governor General's Garden
Party
Rideau Hall, Ottawa
(613) 998-7113
1-800-465-6890

June 26-27, 1999
2000 dates to be announced
National Capital Dragon Boat
Race Festival
Rideau Canoe Club, Mooney's Bay
(613) 238-7711

June 26 to July 4, 2000
Canada Day – Millennium
Celebrations
(613) 239-5000
1-800-465-1867

June 29 to July 4, 1999
June 28 to July 2, 2000
June 27 to July 2, 2001
Unisong
Youth choirs from across Canada
Various venues around Ottawa-
Hull
(613) 234-3360

June 30 to August 2, 1999
2000 dates to be announced
Festival Canada
National Arts Centre and
Jacques-Cartier Park
(613) 947-7000 information
(613) 755-1111 tickets

Strawberry picking season

JULY
To August 2, 1999
2000 dates to be announced
Festival Canada
National Arts Centre, Jacques-
Cartier Park
(613) 947-7000 information
(613) 755-1111 tickets

July 1
Canada Day
Parliament Hill, Major's Hill
Park, Jacques-Cartier Park,
World Exchange Plaza Terrace,
Mackenzie King Estate, Walter
Baker Park, Cumberland
Heritage Village Museum and
your neighbourhood
(613) 239-5000
1-800-465-1867

To July 4, 1999
Unisong
Youth choirs from across Canada
Various venues around Ottawa-
Hull
(613) 234-3360

To July 4, 2000
Canada Day – Millennium
Celebrations
(613) 239-5000
1-800-465-1867

July 8-11, 1999
July 6-9, 2000
Buckingham en Fête
Downtown Buckingham
(819) 281-7732 · 986-4204

July 8-11, 1999
July 7-10, 2000
Ottawa Citizen Bluesfest
Confederation Park and area
nightclubs
(613) 233-8798

July 10, 1999
July 8, 2000
CHEO Teddy Bear Picnic
Rideau Hall, Ottawa
(613) 998-7113

July 14-18, 1999
Mid-July, 2000
Capital Classic Show Jumping
Tournament
National Capital Equestrian
Park, Nepean
(613) 829-6925

July 14-24, 2001
IVᵉ jeux de la francophonie
Hull
(613) 749-5389

July 16-25, 1999
July 15-24, 2000
Ottawa International Jazz
Festival
Confederation Park and area
nightclubs
(613) 241-2633

July 18, 1999
2000 date to be announced
Open-Air Art and Crafts Sale
Andrew Haydon Park, Nepean
(613) 727-6652

July 24 to August 7, 1999
July 22 to August 4, 2000
Ottawa Chamber Music Festival
Various churches downtown
(613) 234-8008

July 25, 1999
July 23, 2000
Flower Celebration
Mackenzie King Estate, Gatineau
Park
(819) 827-2020

July 30-31, 1999
Glengarry Highland Games
Kenyon Agricultural Grounds,
Maxville
(613) 527-2876

July 31 to August 3, 1999
2000 dates to be announced
Ottawa International Busker
Festival
Sparks Street Mall, Ottawa
(613) 730-2353

July 31, August 4, 7, 11, 14, 1999
2000 dates to be announced
The Casino Sound of Light
International Fireworks
Competition
Leamy Lake, Leamy Lake Park
(819) 771-3389
1-888-429-3389

AUGUST
To August 2, 1999
2000 dates to be announced
Festival Canada
National Arts Centre and
Jacques-Cartier Park
(613) 947-7000 information
(613) 755-1111 tickets

To August 3, 1999
2000 dates to be announced
Ottawa International Busker
Festival
Sparks Street Mall, Ottawa
(613) 730-2353

To August 7, 1999
To August 4, 2000
Ottawa Chamber Music Festival
Various churches downtown
(613) 234-8008

August 4-5, 2000
August 3-4, 2001
Glengarry Highland Games
Kenyon Agricultural Grounds,
Maxville
(613) 527-2876

August 4, 7, 11, 14, 1999
2000 dates to be announced
The Casino Sound of Light
International Fireworks
Competition
Leamy Lake, Leamy Lake Park
(819) 771-3389
1-888-429-3389

August 6-8, 1999
August 4-6, 2000
Ghost Walk
Mackenzie King Estate, Gatineau
Park
(819) 827-2020

August 6-8, 1999
August 4-6, 2000
Fête de l'été d'Aylmer
Family activities and classic car
show
Parc de la Marina, Aylmer
(819) 684-9406

August 12-15, 1999
2000 dates to be announced
Navan Fair
Navan Fairgrounds, Navan
(613) 835-2766

August 19-29, 1999
2000 dates to be announced
Central Canada Exhibition
Lansdowne Park, Ottawa
(613) 237-7222

August 22, 1999
August 20, 2000
Garden Party
Mackenzie King Estate, Gatineau
Park
(819) 827-2020

August 27-29, 1999
August 25-27, 2000
CKCU Ottawa Folk Festival
Britannia Park, Ottawa
(613) 230-8234

August 27-29, 1999
2000 dates to be announced
Canadian Grand Masters
Fiddling Championship
Nepean Sportsplex and
Centrepoint Theatre
(613) 592-2495
(613) 727-6650

Late August – dates to be
announced
Cornwall Lift Off Hot Air
Balloon Festival
Cornwall
(613) 933-8973

SEPTEMBER
September 3-6, 1999
September 1-4, 2000
Gatineau Hot Air Balloon
Festival
La Baie Park, Gatineau
(819) 243-2330

September 4-6, 1999
September 2-4, 2000
Urban Music Festival
Astrolabe Theatre, Ottawa
(613) 755-1111

September 5-6, 1999
September 3-4, 2000
Labour Day
Folk music, corn husking, games
Mackenzie King Estate, Gatineau
Park
(819) 827-2020

September 18-19, 1999
September 16-17, 2000
Fall Fair
Upper Canada Village,
Morrisburg
1-800-437-2233

September 19, 1999
2000 date to be announced
Terry Fox Run
Call for the location of the run in
your community.
1-888-836-9786

September 25-26,
October 2-3, 9-11, 1999
September 23-24, September
30-October 1, October 7-9,
2000
Fall Rhapsody
Gatineau Park
(819) 827-2020

September 26, 1999
September 24, 2000
Word on the Street
ByWard Market, Ottawa
Celebration of the written word
(613) 722-5677

Apple picking season

Dates to be announced
Rural Ramble
Self-guided driving tour of
Ottawa Valley farms
(613) 732-4364
1-800-757-6580

2000 date to be announced
Celebration of the Trans Canada
Trail
www.tctrail.ca
1-800-465-3636

Dates to be announced
Agri-Tour Weekend
Self-guided driving tour of
Lower Ottawa Valley farms
1-800-361-7439

OCTOBER
October 1-31
Saunders Farm Haunted
Log Barns and Hayrides
Munster
(613) 838-5440

October 2-3, 9-11, 1999
October 1, October 7-9, 2000
Fall Rhapsody
Gatineau Park
(819) 827-2020

October 9-11, 1999
October 7-9, 2000
Applefest
Cumberland Heritage Village
Museum, Cumberland
(613) 833-3059

October 10-11, 1999
October 8-9, 2000
Fall Harvest Celebration
Agriculture Museum, Ottawa
(613) 991-3044

October 10-11, 1999
October 8-9, 2000
Thanksgiving
Mackenzie King Estate, Gatineau
Park
(819) 827-2020

October 16-17, 23-24, 30-31, 1999
October 14-15, 21-22, 28-29, 2000
Halloween Ghost Walk
Cumberland Heritage Village
Museum, Cumberland
(613) 833-3059

October 21-24, 1999
2000 dates to be announced
Student Animation Festival of
Ottawa
National Archives of Canada,
Ottawa
(613) 232-8769

October 31
Halloween Wave Swim
Kanata Leisure Centre & Wave
Pool
(613) 591-WAVE

Apple picking season

NOVEMBER
Date to be announced
Christmas in the City
Tree lighting, skating, enter-
tainment
Walter Baker Park, Kanata
(613) 592-4291 ext. 209

Date to be announced
Kanata Holidays Parade
(613) 592-8343

DECEMBER
Christmas in the Country
Saunders Farm, Munster
(613) 838-5440

To December 24
A Traditional Christmas
Upper Canada Village,
Morrisburg
1-800-437-2233

December 3, 1999 to January 3, 2000
December 2000
Christmas Lights Across Canada
Parliament Hill and
Confederation Boulevard
(613) 239-5000
1-800-465-1867

December 4-23, 1999
December 2-21, 2000
Old Fashioned Christmas
Cumberland Heritage Village
Museum, Cumberland
(613) 833-3059

December 26-31
Children's Festival Annual
Pantomime
Canadian Museum of Nature,
Ottawa
(613) 566-4700
1-800-263-4433

December 31
New Year's Eve Family Fun
Ben Franklin Place, Nepean
(613) 727-6641

December 31-January 1
New Year's Eve Children's Gala
New Year's Eve party and sleep-
over
Cosmic Adventures, Gloucester
(613) 742-8989

Dates to be announced
The Nutcracker
All-new Nutcracker for the 1999
season
National Arts Centre, Ottawa
(613) 947-7000

Sites
INDEX
(main listing given first)

GENERAL INDEX